A Path to

Self-Transformation

Through **Healthy Living:**

An Introduction to New Food Habits and Nutrition with a
Step Forward to Mindfulness in a Slow and Steady Process
to a Healthy Shape

S R Nakarmi

Dedication

To my beloved master SSSB, my life would not have been the same if I had not found you along the journey. Today you are not with us physically but your shadow and grace are always upon me. You are in me and I am in you. I love you, Baba!

Special gratitude and thanks to my sisters Anita, Sunita, Lali, Sangeeta, and Sabu, for always being there for me and supporting me ALONG every step of my life. You girls are my backbone and heroes. I love you all!

To my parents for bringing me here to this planet where I am able to express everything, I want to through my physical body, for raising me, and for educating me in the right way with humility.

And to my husband and my dearest son—you have been my life's light. Thank you both for loving me the way a woman and a mother hope for.

I love you all from the bottom of my heart.

About the Author

I am a resident of the picturesque landscapes of Western Australia. I am an individual with a diverse range of interests and passions that have shaped my life's journey. From a young age, my love for singing and writing illuminated my path, instilling in them a deep appreciation for creativity and self-expression during my teenage years.

Over the course of decades, I have immersed myself in the world of home and garden improvements, turning spaces into captivating sanctuaries that reflected my innovative spirit.

While my focus remained on sustainable fashion through a side business, I embarked on an eye-opening spiritual pilgrimage overseas in the year 2000, leading to a profound shift in my perspective.

With a curiosity for the world and its nourishment, I delved into the realm of food in my 20s, fostering a keen awareness of proper nutrition and its profound impact on my overall well-being.

My insatiable thirst for knowledge has been an unwavering driving force throughout my life. Exploring diverse subjects, from nutrition and nature - the human mind and the laws of the universe, I ventured into the captivating realm of neuroscience. This newfound passion enriched my understanding of spirituality, unveiling its profound connection to the inner workings of the brain.

In my cherished "ME TIME," I embrace a diverse array of activities, fostering my well-roundedness. Yoga, exercise, meditation, painting, writing, gardening, and watching inspirational documentaries all contribute to my personal growth and inner harmony.

My reverence for spirituality, the world's creation, and the language of love propel my life's journey. Influenced by my spiritual master, SSSB, and the wisdom of Sir David Attenborough.

I am a lifelong learner committed to growth, development, and self-improvement. My graceful navigation through life is inspired by the wonders of human experience and the limitless boundaries of intellectual exploration.

Table of Contents

Insight

For the past 33 years, I have looked in the mirror every morning and asked myself: If today were the last day of my life, would I want to do what I am about to do today? And whenever the answer has been "No" for too many days in a row, I know I need to change something.–Steve Jobs

Steve Jobs is someone that I admire greatly. He was a mere mortal who achieved remarkable feats in his short lifetime. I am not saying that he was perfect, but it was his openness and honesty about his mistakes and fallibility that made him a great teacher; even more so after his death.

He was not afraid of change and making tough decisions. It is this courage that I would like you to borrow from him. This book implores you to be true to yourself and to ask yourself the tough questions about your life and about your physical, mental, and emotional health. It asks you to dig deep within and make these changes for you and nobody else.

One's physical health is determined at conception when the sperm fertilizes the ovum and the chromosomes are merged. The genetic codes from both parents create a blueprint for the fetus and the potential human body that will eventually breathe the air of this amazing planet. Many of us disregard this integral aspect of our present health and how it informs some of the challenges we may face in life, not understanding that they have had their genesis in our first home— our mother's womb.

If you are reading this book, it is obvious that you have arrived at a juncture in your life where you are beginning your search for greater meaning. Possibly, you have encountered a physical, mental, emotional, or spiritual crisis that has propelled you to look for solutions.

Let's begin this journey with the wisdom of the sages. You must first recognize that you are a perfect spirit being having a human experience. We are born with a blank slate and create our reality from the innate raw materials that we incarnate with. As individuals, we are bombarded by a host of environments and experiences that influence the way we interact with the world and with others. Psychology calls this the nature versus nurture debate. In reality, we are a complex mixture of nature and nurture, and the path to transformation is to embrace all aspects of ourselves.

That being said, this is a conversation, though one-sided, about how you as an individual can recreate your life by making a few dramatic changes. It is not focused on just one aspect of health but rather sees the individual as a holistic entity comprising many layers. For any significant change to be made, we will need to delve into all the variables that have shaped you as an individual. For example, we cannot look only at the physical body and make cosmetic changes; we need to examine the psychological and emotional aspects of eating habits that affect your physical appearance, as well. We will look at what has shaped you into the person you are today to get to the heart of why you make certain decisions about your health. We will need to peel away the layers that you have gathered around you as protection to hide you from that which haunts you today.

As we delve into the complexity of the human experience, we will begin to view ourselves as multi-dimensional beings with our physical, emotional, and spiritual selves entangled in an intricate web. It takes a lot of honest introspection and soul-searching to unearth the reasons for any dis-ease in our bodies.

There are thousands of self-help books written by brilliant writers who have gone on these reflective journeys before me, and they have offered insights that have helped me on my quest for a healthier mind, body, and spirit. I am offering you my personal lessons together with valuable insights from the great masters that have come before me.

The broad scope of this book is to unearth the various aspects that constitute "healthy living," and how this is achievable in small baby steps that anyone can begin. Nutrition and exercise are integral aspects of health and will be a focus. One's inner landscape and interiority will be a focal point of this book because, in my opinion, our thoughts can create chaos and stress which in turn create dis-ease and imbalance.

Another key focus area will be fertility, pre-and-post natal health in women, and a look at abnormalities in newborns. It is impossible to divorce myself from the reality that I am writing this from the perspective and experience of a woman. Millions of men and women the world over face unrealistic expectations of them to fit into a certain ideal of what is desirable physically, mentally, and emotionally.

History was written by men, and it is a known fact that women have been disempowered for a very long time. I will explore, in some detail, how women have fallen into the age-old trap of allowing themselves to judge themselves so harshly because they were seen as a commodity in the marriage market for millennia. Even though I write this book as an empowered woman, it speaks to people of all genders who are searching for solutions.

The purpose of this book is to promote a healthier lifestyle. My mission is to provide information and resources to help people lead a healthier and more balanced life. It can be encouraging and empowering for readers to access information about the right foods if they have the correct information provided by someone with greater experience. Thus, the knowledge and information that I have gathered over the last 22 years will help readers achieve in-depth knowledge for their needs.

In my own personal quest, I have accumulated wisdom and insight into understanding people's habits and the obstacles they may face as they navigate this difficult journey to self-transformation. I have thoughtfully researched and created six reasons why we would want to change our lives for the better and how we can achieve this goal by taking slow and steady steps for a lifelong result. This book does not only explain what you should eat but also guides you on how you should feel, think, and act to create a healthier life that can improve productivity, happiness, and contentment.

Another imperative takeaway from this book is to alert the reader that time is finite. We are eternal beings having a finite human experience. That entails an undisclosed period of time in which we have to master many lessons in a fallible and fragile body that we inhabit. 'Time and tide wait for no man," says the old adage, and that applies to our human body. What you put in is what you get out. If you put junk in, you will pay the price of reduced energy output and the threat of disease. Time is not on our side. It hovers over us—this invisible, colossal timer, similar to the lives we get on a computer game: tick-tock, tick-tock—until we expire. We have to beat time at its own game by finding ways to extend our play and prolong our lifespan.

Additionally, this book also focuses on changing our mindsets by removing negative qualities we may carry. This book will end with tips and guidance on Reflection and Quietness, leaving readers with a peaceful mind.

Self-Reflection and Realization

Don't be satisfied with stories, how things have gone with others. Unfold your own myth.–Rumi

The world is filled with myths and legends; of Gods and deities, heaven and hell. As Rumi says, each of us has to figure out for ourselves what it means to know who we are or what we are made of. We need to ask ourselves the pertinent questions: Who am I? Where do I come from? What is my purpose? For each of us, the answers will be different. We have to find meaning that resonates with our souls.

Self-Reflection is about reflecting on ourselves; the good and bad habits we maintain that have brought us to where we are now. You are holding this book in your hands and reading these words because you know that you need to change something in your life.

Self-realization refers to the process of becoming aware of one's true nature, potential, and purpose in life. It involves gaining a deeper understanding of oneself, including one's values, beliefs, thoughts, emotions, strengths, weaknesses, and desires. Self-realization often involves undertaking a deliberate journey of self-discovery and personal growth, where we strive to align our actions and choices with our authentic selves. Realization of oneself involves developing a holistic perspective of one's identity, including the physical, mental, emotional, and spiritual aspects of one's being.

Both self-reflection and self-realization are interconnected, and are also often intertwined. When we engage in the process of self-realization, we gain a clearer understanding of who we are and what we want in life. This, in turn, contributes to deeper self-reflection and realization of oneself as a whole person with unique qualities, potential, and sense of purpose.

It's important to note that self-reflection and realization of oneself are subjective experiences that can vary from person to person. The paths to self-discovery and personal growth are highly individual, and they can involve various practices, such as introspection, self-reflection, meditation, therapy, journaling, or seeking guidance from mentors or spiritual teachers. Ultimately, the process of self-reflection and realization of oneself is a lifelong journey that unfolds gradually over time.

I have spent the last 22 years of my life properly engaged in both of these endeavors. It has taken me through great personal growth. In my case, I found myself a Great Master along the way, whose dedication and commitment to his society influenced me to dig deeper into myself to understand others' needs.

I found that understanding and helping others brought me closer to myself and my purpose in life. It also taught me compassion, and the importance of putting others first. I am constantly learning from my society and surroundings, stumbling and picking up from where I have erred; such is the nature of humans.

I invite you on this journey of self-realization with me, to undertake this journey together, unravel and unmask who you are, and find out what has led you to this point in your life. This book is not just about becoming healthier in your body; it's more about your internal landscape and aligning your values with your purpose.

Self-reflection involves going within and getting to know who you really are at your core. What motivates you? What are your values? What makes you who you are? We come to realize that we are not just the body or the mind and that there is something intangible that makes us unique. Some people call this the "soul" or "inner spirit."

Although this book is about health and well-being, I believe that real well-being comes from self-realization and knowing oneself. When a person is disconnected from their true nature their psyche becomes fragmented. This results in problems such as ill health, unhealthy weight gain, or extreme weight loss.

Before you embark on your health odyssey, I believe that it is essential to make this a holistic one, where you make connections between body, mind, and spirit. I have made elaborate attempts to focus on helping you find out what makes you tick. You cannot make any real progress until you experience self-realization.

This book is divided into two parts. In the first part, I explore the six reasons why people want to make a change. In the second part, I offer the steps you can take to make these changes.

Part 1:

Six Reasons Why
We Want to Change for the Better

Reason 1:
Jealousy and Insecurity

The only thing you have in your life is time. If you invest that time in yourself to have great experiences that are going to enrich you, then you can't possibly lose. —Steve Jobs

Many of us are envious of the men and women we watch on the big screen, on television, on the runways of New York and Milan, or the faces and bodies that stare at us from magazine covers and billboards. We are envious of their seemingly-perfect bodies and beautiful faces. These famous actors, actresses, and models offer a physical perfection that we yearn for but can never quite achieve.

Women are not the only ones affected by the popular belief in a perfect human specimen. Amongst males, there is the belief nowadays that being a short or small man is not ideal. If you are carrying too much weight, you are considered unattractive. Tall men with defined musculature are lauded and celebrated. There is a tendency to view looking like anything else as "other," lesser, and unattractive.

Our ideals are reflected in our popular culture and benchmarks are set by people that are in the limelight for various reasons. They become the icons and beacons by which we measure our own self-image. There are several reasons why people may feel envious of others with slimmer bodies. Many cultures place a high value on being slender, associating it with beauty, success, and self-discipline. As a result, people may feel pressure to conform to these norms and may feel envious of those who are able to achieve a slimmer body.

If we compare the present time to 20 years ago, there have been a lot of changes in people's awareness around issues of health and wellness. This can be attributed to globalization and social media. We find more and more people are interested in plant-based vegetarianism or veganism. People the world over are cutting down on meat, becoming more active, and engaging in meditation. As a result of this awareness, those who don't believe in any of the above are considered uneducated or ignorant. Thus, a lack of interest in this new type of awareness makes others jealous and insecure.

Many people still equate thinness with beauty and success, and this has contributed to the rise of eating disorders and body dysmorphia in many cultures. However, there is also growing awareness of the dangers of promoting an unrealistic and unhealthy beauty standard, and efforts are being made to promote body positivity and acceptance of all body types.

I believe that a healthy lifestyle requires you to be mindful of your diet and your physical activity. Your awareness of your diet and regular exercise should be the foundation of your health plan. Ultimately, your goal should be to achieve and maintain your ideal weight and wellness of your mind.

People who struggle with their weight or body image may feel envious of others who appear to have achieved their ideal body size and shape. Personal insecurities creep in when we lack the discipline to make the changes we need to for a number of reasons. There are many reasons why people feel insecure about their bodies, and it can vary from person to person and from time to time.

Some common factors that contribute to body insecurities include the following.

- Societal pressure and unrealistic beauty standards

- Comparing ourselves to others

- Past experiences of bullying or negative comments

- Trauma or abuse

- Personal experiences

- Genetics

In some cases, we are likely to envy others who have slim bodies because we associate slimness with good health. However, it's important to remember that body size and health are not always correlated. Personally, I have known a number of really skinny male friends who became chronically ill with heart problems and diabetes.

It is a misnomer to judge people as being healthy simply because they are thin. Having a thin body does not necessarily mean one is healthier than another, as everything needs balance. Being overweight does not necessarily mean you are unhealthy, either, as long as you are active and eat a balanced diet. Likewise, having a thin body only equates to good health if you are getting proper nutrients and exercise.

Some of us may also feel envious of others with slim bodies simply because we are comparing ourselves to others and feel that our own body falls short in some way. This can create a sense of competition or even resentment towards those who appear to have a more "ideal" body size and shape.

You may have felt embarrassed choosing a size 18 or 20 when a customer next to you grabbed a size 8 or 10. Constantly facing situations like this may have made you insecure or somewhat jealous. These feelings of insecurity can have a damaging impact on your self-esteem and sense of worth. It can lead to feelings of inadequacy and damage your mental and emotional well-being. However, I understand why you feel the way you do, and please know that there is a solution for you. If you want to change your situation and be proud of your decisions, you can (and I will show you how).

Overall, the envy of others can be driven by a complex combination of cultural norms, personal insecurities, health concerns, and social comparison. It's important to remember that everyone's body is unique and that there is no one "right" way to look or feel. However, if you truly feel insecure about your weight then it is time to acknowledge that you may need to take some action. When you look in the mirror and see for yourself that there is an inner truth that does not allow you to accept yourself, then perhaps it is time to change what you do not like. Make an effort to get out of your comfort zone and challenge yourself. Don't be afraid to make mistakes, as they are a part of the learning process. Believe in yourself and realize that you are a capable human with all the tools to achieve anything you put your mind to.

The medical community is constantly making links between obesity and chronic diseases. This viewpoint has convinced us that being overweight is undesirable and that slender people are indeed healthier. However, more recent research has shown that this might not always be the case. Although being overweight can increase the risk of certain diseases, it is not always the cause. In some cases, lifestyle choices such as lack of exercise and poor diet can be more to blame than weight.

Reason 2:
Low Self-Esteem

Your time is limited, so don't waste it living someone else's life. Don't be trapped by dogma—which is living the results of other people's thinking. DON'T LET THE NOISE OF OTHER PEOPLE'S OPINIONS DROWN OUT YOUR OWN INNER VOICE. –Steve Jobs

Many of us are oblivious to the many issues that affect our self-esteem as we grow from infancy through childhood and into adolescence and adulthood. There are thousands of encounters that may have impacted how you view yourself today and for the unconscious reasons behind the decisions you make about your current health and wellness. A few nasty words from your parents or other significant people in your life about you eating too much or looking "fat" may continue to overshadow and impede any progress you try to make.

I am not an expert on the psychological effects of low self-esteem or trauma, but I believe that we need to understand the reasons behind the decisions we make around our health choices. Within our subconscious minds there are many experiences that impact how we interact with the world and that directly affect our personality.

Our personality and perceptions about ourselves impinge on how we nurture ourselves, what we eat, and our values about physical fitness. This book is not just about healthy eating, it is about creating a healthy body through a thorough understanding of your external and internal worlds. Focusing only on your physical body will yield results for a short period of time, but focusing on your overall physical, mental, emotional, and spiritual health will last you a lifetime.

Our self-esteem influences all our interactions and relationships with others. It has a direct bearing on our social interactions in the workplace, as well as at home. At home or work, our low self-esteem affects what we eat. You may eat cheese sandwiches with bacon and sugary drinks while your colleagues eat a healthy salad or vegetarian dish. You may want to sit in a corner, away from your colleagues, to feel more comfortable, or try to avoid them at every opportunity. Your self-esteem inadvertently creates barriers for you to interact healthily in your environment, and it impacts the choices you make.

Poor eating habits may result in an unhealthy body, and people can become cagey and self-conscious when that happens. Overweight people can become extra sensitive and paranoid that everyone is looking at them and judging them, even though this may be far from true. They may begin to feel this way when their self-esteem has hit rock bottom.

I do not mean to imply that people are not guilty of judging others in that way, but in all likelihood, the extent may be exaggerated in one's mind. Despite how well people dress or look, tons of people will have negative views of others, and mock or laugh at others who do not conform to certain standards.

It is normal for overweight people to feel excluded in certain circles or groups. They may feel excluded when a group of people talks about healthy food, workout routines, or a healthy shape. As a result of not being fit or healthy, they may be hesitant to participate in certain conversations.

Low self-esteem can have a significant impact on weight, eating, and exercise behaviors. According to a study by Hagger-Johnson, Roberts, and Boniface (2013), individuals with low self-esteem are more likely to engage in unhealthy eating behaviors, such as binge eating and emotional eating, which can lead to weight gain and obesity.

Moreover, low self-esteem can also lead to a lack of motivation to exercise, as individuals may feel that they are not capable of achieving their fitness goals or that they do not deserve to be healthy. According to a study by Sonstroem and Morgan (1989), individuals with low self-esteem are less likely to engage in physical activity and more likely to engage in sedentary behaviors.

In addition, low self-esteem can lead to a negative body image, which can further impact eating and exercise behaviors. Those with negative body image may engage in restrictive eating behaviors such as extreme dieting or skipping meals in an attempt to achieve their desired body weight or shape. Similarly, individuals with negative body image may avoid exercise or physical activity, as they may feel self-conscious or embarrassed about their appearance. It is essential to address the underlying issues of low self-esteem to promote healthy lifestyle behaviors and improve overall well-being.

Low self-esteem can have various roots that are often intertwined and complex. You become a product of your environment, together with your innate sense of self.

Reason 3:
Fertility

Ask any doting parent about their children and you will see their face and eyes light up as they talk about them. The same goes for people speaking about their pups or kittens or birds. Children offer the opportunity for us to look at ourselves and try to be better people, to demonstrate love and affection, and to try harder at making a success of our lives so that we may give them a good life.

Not all of us are destined to have children or choose the path of being a parent, but I would assert that there are more people who would love to be parents than those who don't. Research suggests that being overweight can have negative effects on fertility in both men and women, so if you are a young adult who yearns to have a child of your own someday, or you are perhaps already a parent, it is crucial to have a healthy body and not carry excess weight (Mayo Clinic, 2022).

I have encountered many young adults in my family and my work who have married with the intention of having a baby right away, but many of them have spent years trying without success. Some of them have been advised by their obstetrician or gynecologist to lose the extra pounds before they can begin trying for a baby.

For women, being overweight can disrupt the delicate balance of hormones that regulate the menstrual cycle and ovulation, potentially leading to infertility. Additionally, excess weight can increase the risk of conditions such as polycystic ovary syndrome (PCOS), which can also negatively impact fertility (Legro et al., 2013).

PCOS is a complex hormonal disorder that affects women of reproductive age. Doctors cannot pinpoint the exact cause of PCOS, but it is thought to be caused by a combination of genetic, environmental, and lifestyle factors.

Some of the known risk factors for PCOS include insulin resistance, obesity, a family history of PCOS, and high levels of androgens (male hormones) in the body. Insulin resistance is believed to play a significant role in the development of PCOS, as it leads to high levels of insulin in the body, which in turn can stimulate the ovaries to produce more androgens.

There is also evidence to suggest that exposure to certain environmental toxins, such as bisphenol A (BPA), may contribute to the development of PCOS. Additionally, stress, poor diet, and lack of physical activity may also be risk factors for PCOS. Personally, I believe that PCOS is a modern disease created by our lifestyle, scientific farming methods, processed foods, plastic packaging, hormones in our meat products, birth control pills, and even the clothes we wear.

It is important to note that while the exact cause of PCOS is not known, there are effective treatments available to help manage the symptoms of the condition. If you suspect you may have PCOS, it is important to consult with a healthcare professional for diagnosis and treatment.

Getting closer to a healthy weight before conception increases the chance of the baby being healthy at birth and into adulthood. Being significantly overweight can pose many problems during pregnancy, and there are many complications that may arise. Some of the complications include (Better Health, 2012):

- miscarriage

- stillbirth

- high blood pressure

- pre-eclampsia

- gestational diabetes

- Cesarean birth

The infants that obese or overweight mothers give birth to may have a greater risk of certain diseases. They are more likely to be at risk of becoming obese in childhood or be at risk of other diseases such as heart issues (Kureshi et al, 2022).

Research shows that women who go on a weight loss program and make an effort to lose just a little weight show improved chances of fertility. During pregnancy, women are encouraged to continue to follow a healthy diet and engage in some light exercise, such as walking. Personally, I have found that eating a well-balanced diet, and not "eating for two" during my own pregnancy helped me to recover much faster after giving birth.

It's important to alert you to the risks that can occur during pregnancy if you are overweight or obese (ACOG, 2023):

- Gestational hypertension—This is high blood pressure that can occur during the second and third trimesters and can compromise the health of the mother and the fetus.

- Pre-eclampsia—This can occur around five or six months in the second and third trimesters, or even after birth. It can lead to kidney or liver failure. In some rare cases, seizures, heart attacks, and strokes can happen. Pre-eclampsia can also affect the placenta and the growth of the baby.

- Gestational diabetes—Many women who carry excess weight are diagnosed with gestational diabetes, which refers to high blood sugar levels which can impact the baby's birth weight (making it high). This alters the chance of a natural birth and increases the mother's chances of having a Cesarean birth.

- Obstructive sleep apnea—Sleep apnea occurs when a person stops breathing for short periods during sleep. During pregnancy, women experience sleep apnea, which can cause extreme tiredness. This can increase the risk of high blood pressure, pre-eclampsia, and heart and lung problems.

- If you are overweight during pregnancy, there is a risk that your baby may have congenital heart defects or neural tube defects. It is also possible that belly fat may prevent the doctor from seeing any problems with the fetus' anatomy during a routine prenatal ultrasound scan.

In men, being overweight can also affect hormone levels and sperm quality, potentially leading to decreased fertility. A meta-analysis of 21 studies found that overweight and obese men were more likely to have a lower sperm count and reduced sperm motility compared to men of normal weight (Sermondade et al., 2013).

Therefore, the importance of a healthy weight for both males and females to fertility is evident.

Reason 4:
Future Consequences and Finances

Remembering that you are going to die is the best way I know to avoid the trap of thinking you have something to lose. You are already naked. There is no reason not to follow your heart. –Steve Jobs

If you are a parent of young children, you may have realized the consequences of your life journey ending earlier than you planned. You start thinking about becoming a healthier version of yourself because you do not want to leave behind those who are still vulnerable, dependent, or who mean the world to you.

If you were diagnosed with a terminal illness, you may be replaced by a stepmother or father who would raise your children and live with your partner instead of you. Not every stepmother or father is mean and nasty, but what if this particular stepparent falls into that offensive and cruel category and makes your children's lives miserable? There are countless unknown possibilities following your demise, which is terrifying to consider.

When you become a parent, your children are your heart. They are a part of you walking the Earth. It is your responsibility to be as healthy as you can be so that they can enjoy the best of you. Being overweight and leading a sedentary lifestyle is not good for your overall health, nor is it a healthy example for your children. Your children were brought into existence by your will and choice, and you owe them your physical, healthy presence in their lives until they can stand on their own two feet.

The key to maintaining a healthy mind, body, and spirit is to practice mindfulness. Being mindful is living consciously and thinking about your actions and how they impact yourself and others. A mindful person will live in gratitude for each moment and make decisions that are beneficial to all aspects of his or her physical, mental, emotional, and spiritual health, as well as to those around them.

As a mature adult, you bear a great deal of responsibility for your home, family, and pets. Having a home and a family incurs a lot of expenses, and this entails you being in peak health to maintain a job to support your family. Children also need the presence of a physically and mentally healthy mother and father to develop aspects of their personality so that they can become the best version of themselves. The financial aspect of running a thriving household requires us to take care of ourselves. It is important for us to practice self-care. Sometimes we get so caught up in the rat race that we forget we need to recharge our batteries so that we don't run on empty.

Many of us do not pay attention to what we eat during the day whilst we are on the go. We guzzle many cups of coffee and miss meals, or guzzle a hotdog for lunch, but all these little bad habits eventually take their toll on our bodies and result in all kinds of diseases.

We spend the majority of our time focused on our jobs and undergo high levels of stress. Stress hormones play havoc in the body and create dis-ease. Our bodies begin to strain under the pressure we are putting on them, and we can experience health scares.

If you have a heart attack, cancer, or stroke, can you imagine the cost of months of treatments and recuperation? Below is a list of considerations.

- Heart attack: $21,500 on average for about five days in the hospital, even with insurance coverage

- A cancer diagnosis is $42,000

- Stroke rehabilitation is approximately $70,601 and $27,473

- Chest x-rays

- Echocardiogram

- Magnetic Resonance Imaging (MRI)

- Computed Tomography (CT) Scans

- Heart stent

- Emergency room visit

- Bypass surgery

- Intravenous medication

- Bloodwork and lab tests

- Room and care charges

It could mean quitting your job and putting your career in jeopardy as you would be losing many work hours. Think about your kids' school and their expenses and how you would cope. All these expenses could quickly add up, leaving families struggling to pay bills and living in a state of financial instability. This could lead to more serious issues, such as debt and poverty. These issues can have a lasting and detrimental effect on a family, both emotionally and financially.

Reason 5:
Fear

Remembering that I'll be dead soon is the most important tool I've ever encountered to help me make the big choices in life. Because almost everything—all external expectations, all pride, all fear of embarrassment or failure—these things just fall away in the face of death, leaving only what is truly important. –Steve Jobs

A fear of dying is one of the greatest motivators for those of us that want to get healthier, although we all know that death is the only certainty we have when we are born. It is only when we are faced with the prospect of losing it all that we are pushed out of our comfort zone. All our bad habits and stupid decisions will eventually kill us. I want you to be afraid, so afraid that you have an epiphany and begin your journey to wellness. I want you to know that you are a mortal, and that you have a finite time on this planet, in this body. If you continue on the same trajectory that you are on, you may die a premature death and leave your family and friends behind

At the end of the day, Steve Jobs had billions in the bank, but it all meant nothing. What people remember about you is how you made them feel. Suppose you receive a negative medical test result. The disease may cause your death. You have to endure months of treatment, hospitalization, and pain. In addition to physical suffering, your family will also suffer emotionally from your illness because they simply cannot watch you go through that horrible chapter of your life. Your innocent children would be subjected to significant turmoil during this time due to the emotional and financial hardship.

This painful episode in your life will strip you of your pride. You will begin to understand what is important. Time will be your greatest enemy. You will want to spend it with your family. Only when you are close to death will you fully value life and love. You will dwell on all the experiences you have not had and dream that you could have done it all differently. You would not want the illness to bring you suffering and you would not want to become dependent or be a burden to your spouse and children.

As much as you want to spare your family the pain, months of suffering will follow, and your illness will bring chaos to the lives of your vulnerable children who have not yet become independent. Their hearts would be broken by loneliness and despair when you leave them behind. I want you to take yourself through the pain of seeing your dependent children orphaned. Visualize all of this happening and feel the tears of regret cascade down your cheeks, because if you do not change your habits, this is a possibility.

Hence, if you think this could happen to you, you may want to change your lifestyle. If so, you have come to the right place; there is light ahead of you.

Here Is the Flip Side of How Fear Can Limit Your Personal Growth

Fear often stems from a fear of failure or a fear of the unknown. This can lead to a reluctance to take risks or try new things. However, growth and learning often occur outside of our comfort zones, and by avoiding risks, we miss out on valuable opportunities for personal development. You must become comfortable with being uncomfortable if you want to change your present circumstances.

Fear can keep us stuck in our present circumstances and stops us from making the necessary changes in our lives. Whether it's staying in an unfulfilling job, remaining in unhealthy relationships, or avoiding challenging situations, fear can keep us trapped in a state of stagnation and prevent personal growth.

Fear can erode our self-confidence and make us doubt our abilities. When we doubt ourselves and are afraid of failure, we may shy away from pursuing our goals and dreams. Without the confidence to take action and overcome obstacles, personal growth becomes limited.

Growth often requires embracing discomfort and pushing through challenges. However, fear can lead us to avoid uncomfortable situations altogether. By seeking comfort and familiarity, we miss out on opportunities for personal growth and learning.

Overcoming fear is crucial for personal growth. Following are a few strategies that can help you navigate your way through fear and insecurities.

Acknowledge and Understand Your Fears

Recognize what fears are holding you back and try to understand their origins. By gaining insight into your fears, you can start to address them more effectively. This stage of your contemplation must be recorded in your journal.

Challenge Your Limiting Beliefs

Examine the underlying beliefs and assumptions that kick-started your fears. Ask yourself if these fears are rational and realistic. Often, our fears are based on ridiculous assumptions, and by challenging them, we can start to diminish their power.

Take Baby Steps Outside Your Comfort Zone

Start by taking small, manageable steps that will push you a little bit out of your comfort zone. Gradually exposing yourself to new experiences can help you build confidence and extend your comfort zone over time.

Seek Support

Talk to friends, family, or a therapist about your fears and aspirations. Sharing your concerns and receiving support can provide you with encouragement and different perspectives that can help you overcome your fears.

Embrace Failure as a Learning Opportunity

Instead of viewing failure as something to be feared, reframe it as a valuable learning experience. We need to accept that setbacks and mistakes are a natural part of growing and can provide valuable insights for future success.

Remember, personal growth requires courage and a willingness to face your fears. By confronting and overcoming them, you open yourself up to new opportunities and possibilities for self-improvement. Are you ready to take your fear on and change your life? You should be able to answer these questions fearlessly before taking steps forward, and only then you are fully ready for the next journey of your life.

Reason 6:
The Curves and Shape

I want you to know that there is nothing wrong with having a womanly shape or curves. In many cultures, a woman with curves is seen as far more attractive than skinnier women. The problem begins when the curves start to disappear and are replaced by fat. It is this that can cause many diseases and can jeopardize your health. When excess weight becomes an obstacle to your ability to move freely, if you are panting after walking a short distance, or if you cannot keep up with your children, then it is time to realize that you have to make different choices for your health.

It takes a lot of courage to lose even a little weight and step into that new world of diets and exercise. When you think about curves and how you are able to make yourself look attractive, you are trying to fit into a whole different way of being. There are a lot of individuals who would take any measure to make themselves look younger, sexier, and more attractive.

I want to encourage you to take that first step to change your life, to understand that you deserve to have a more enriching life in a physical body that functions better. You have the ability to achieve your goal by eating less or eating healthy food and exercising.

Whatever your reasons for stepping onto this new path, I applaud you for finally doing something for yourself. Although the goal is the same for all of us, often the process can vary since we all are different individuals. It does not matter how you got to this point, as long as we get the desired result.

Besides the health benefits and the prospect of being thinner or more attractive, eating healthier food and shedding the toxic fat from your body will also make you feel better on a personal level. As you transform your form, you will begin to love your body more, and the positive comments from family and friends will take you to an entirely new level of self-acceptance. Thus, you will be inspired to continue your journey and add value to your life. Doing this will give you a deeper understanding of food and its role in your body, more so than most people who have not begun their journey.

Looking at healthy foods at supermarkets will be the first step in your journey. You will begin to pay closer attention to the ingredients in your food. You will shop for more whole foods such as fruits and vegetables. In time, you will start to notice foods that have healing properties, and you will gain a deeper understanding and appreciation of the relationship between you and the plants.

In addition to this, you may gain valuable knowledge about using natural remedies to treat common health issues that you would have been oblivious to previously.

Exercise and meditation may eventually become another part of your daily routine, which is another great path to healing. This is when your journey begins to get serious. Once you reach this level, you can consider yourself a fully-fledged member of the Healthy Living Subculture that you could only have imagined in your dreams.

Part 2:

An Introduction to

New Food Habits and Nutrition
with a Step Forward to
**Mindfulness in a Slow and Steady
Process to
a Healthy Shape**

Step 1—
Start Small

That's been one of my mantras—focus and simplicity. Simple can be harder than complex; you have to work hard to get your thinking clean to make it simple. –
Steve Jobs

Maintaining a healthy body is essential for a fulfilling life. However, most people find it challenging to establish and maintain a healthy lifestyle. One reason for this is the misconception that adopting a healthy lifestyle requires radical changes that can be overwhelming and unsustainable, when in fact, small changes in lifestyle can have a significant impact on overall health.

While maintaining a healthy weight can be an important part of overall health, being thin does not necessarily equate to being healthy. Health is influenced by a wide range of factors, including genetics, exercise, diet, stress levels, sleep habits, and more.

In fact, being too thin can sometimes be a sign of poor health. For example, individuals with eating disorders such as anorexia nervosa may have a very low body weight and experience a range of serious health problems as a result of their disordered eating behaviors. Thus, it is vital to understand your body's requirements through awareness and education about your own body.

Understanding nutrition and its role in your health is what gives you ultimate success. Remember: health is wealth. You only enjoy your wealth when you have good health. Therefore, running around for weight loss pills and products is not something I would suggest to anyone in life.

Developing new and healthy food habits can require a difficult commitment to changing your lifestyle. Thus, mindfulness is an important factor in this process, as it involves being aware of what you are consuming and how it will affect your health. A slow and steady approach to creating healthy habits is the key for you to achieving a healthy shape in the long run.

When to Start? How to Start?

Above is an overview of a few of the baby steps you can take, but the questions remain: How do I begin? When do I get started? These questions might be difficult for you. If getting started is a problem, let's undertake this journey together and follow a simple step-by-step plan.

Five Easy and Practical Steps to a Healthy Shape

Step 1: Detoxifying Your System

For many years you have ingested a lot of food that was damaging to your system. A lot of these substances have accumulated in your body and have caused dis-ease and toxins to form. A bad diet can contribute to the accumulation of toxins in the body through various mechanisms.

One way is by promoting the production of free radicals, which are unstable molecules that can damage cells and tissues. According to a study by Hussain et al. (2020), a diet high in processed foods, saturated fats, and sugars can increase the production of free radicals, leading to oxidative stress and cellular damage.

Another way that a bad diet can lead to the build-up of toxins in the body is by impairing the function of organs responsible for detoxification, such as the liver and kidneys. For example, a diet high in alcohol, sugar, and refined carbohydrates can impair liver function and hinder its ability to eliminate toxins from the body (Kanerva et al., 2019).

Further, it has been found that a diet that is lacking in essential nutrients such as fiber, vitamins, and minerals can disrupt the balance of the gut microbiome, leading to dysbiosis and the buildup of harmful bacteria and toxins in the gut (Gupta et al., 2019).

After researching the build-up of toxins and the way it impacts disease in the body, you must know by now that it is definitely time to detox your system before you begin your health journey. Detoxification is a process that involves removing toxins or harmful substances from the body.

There are many ways to detoxify the body, including dietary changes, eating raw vegetables, vegetable and berry juices, herbs, and fasting from time to time. A study by P. Porawancherdsak and colleagues (2020) investigated the effects of a three-day juice fast on gut microbiota and metabolic markers in healthy adults. The results indicated that the juice fast led to changes in gut microbiota composition and increased insulin sensitivity.

In summary, there is some evidence to suggest that detoxification methods may have potential health benefits. However, more research is needed to fully understand the mechanisms and effectiveness of various detoxification strategies.

At this point, I think that it is important to apprise you of my background as a person of East Asian descent. In the West, where I have been living for the past 20 years, my knowledge and wisdom about food and its power in our bodies went through the roof. This happened especially when I started building my large garden and the serenity, where I enjoyed for over 17 years of my life. I learned the importance of eating natural, if not always organic. I also discovered the impact of food on our physical, mental, and emotional health, along with the laws of nature, which has been an incredible journey, making me a strong advocate for living a healthier lifestyle.

I am more influenced by natural medicine in my life and other tried and tested herbal remedies like Ayurveda that were passed on over many millennia to our present generation. As people from the West traveled to the East, they began to discover a lot of wisdom from the sages about detoxification, cleansing of the body, meditation, prayer, contemplation, and spiritual gathering or devotions.

For detoxification, the method that I would suggest is the following.

My 14-Day Detox Solution for a Healthy Gut

This is a mixture that you must drink first thing in the morning.

- 1 tbsp. of apple cider vinegar

- 1 tbsp. of lemon juice

- A glass of warm water (warm or cold) to drink on an empty stomach every day of the week at least for two weeks.

This can be diluted with more water if it is too sour for you, but it is not recommended that you drink this without water. If it is still difficult to swallow, add half a teaspoon of pure honey. (Make sure the honey you use is wild bee honey, as most farmed honey is sugar-fed to the bees). **Otherwise, it is recommended to drink this mixture without honey since we are taking the first steps to eliminate sugar and fat from the body.** Make sure the water is not too hot when you mix in the apple cider vinegar since it is a bacterial formation and you don't want to kill the important part of the mixture.

After a week, note any changes in your body, not just weight loss. Determine if you:

- feel an improvement in your gut health.

- feel lighter in the stomach or

- were suffering from gas or bloating and felt a reduction in these symptoms.

This drink is specifically for liver detoxification, but research shows it has many other benefits that go far beyond that (Netmed, 2022). However, if you find any discomfort in your stomach or experience gas or bloating which has significantly increased over time, or any other issue after consuming this drink, you should check in with your doctor. It may indicate that you have an underlying health issue that you may not have known of, and these symptoms may be a reaction to your hidden issues.

There are many other detoxification remedies that you can try depending on your preference or your body's resilience. For your detox journey, try the following foods, and try to make these foods a part of your regular diet.

Lemons

A lot of my friends swear by having a glass of hot water with a slice of lemon first thing in the morning as a daily cleanser for the palate and the gut. According to Narayana Health (2013), lemons are loaded with vitamin C, which is an important antioxidant. It is good armor against free radicals in our environment which contribute to illness and disease. It also does wonders for our skin. Other advantages are that it is an alkaline substance that restores the pH balance and flushes out toxins.

Ginger

Ginger is used in the cooking of many Indian and Asian dishes for a reason. It is known to help digestion and combat bloating and nausea, and to reduce gas in the process of digestion. Ginger is also high in antioxidants, which means that it boosts the immune system. Use it in tea or grate it into fresh juice (Narayana Health, 2013).

Garlic

I grew up hearing about the greatness of garlic and its benefits throughout my life. It is recommended to take one to two cloves of raw chopped garlic a day as medication. In spite of this, consuming high quantities of it every day is not really recommended due to its intensity in the spiritual world.

Garlic is supposed to be good for the heart, but I have recently discovered that it is a detoxifying food as well. It is antibacterial, antibiotic, and antiviral. It contains allicin, which promotes the production of white blood cells. It fights toxins in the body. It has long been known for its heart benefits; however, pungent food is also good at detoxifying the body.

Artichokes

These vegetables are packed with antioxidants and fiber, assist in liver function, and digest fatty foods.

Beetroot

Beetroot is rich in iron (red color), magnesium, and vitamin C. It has been hailed by foodies as a superfood, and is beneficial for skin, hair, and in lowering cholesterol. It is also a great food for a liver detox. Consume it in a salad or drink it as a juice.

Green Tea

Any detox plan will require lots of fluids, and having a detox tea is recommended. Chinese green tea has been hailed as the ultimate detox tea. It is packed with antioxidants, and according to Narayana Health (2013), it may protect the liver from fatty liver disease. In spite of its many benefits, green tea is also known for its high caffeine content. Please be mindful of how much green tea you have per day.

Cabbage

In recent years, the cabbage soup diet did its rounds as a weight loss food. Science tells us that cruciferous vegetables such as sprouts, broccoli, and cabbage contain sulforaphane, which assists in detoxing the body. Cabbage has glutathione, which is an antioxidant. Cabbage is also known to heal gastritis and ulcers.

Fresh Fruit and Raw Vegetables

Smoothies have become the choice of many young adults who have very little time for having real meals during the day. There are numerous smoothie makers on the market and smoothie recipes available. They allow people who find it hard to eat fruit to have their daily intake in a form that is easy to consume. The fruit smoothie can be combined with many other ingredients, as well, like seeds, nuts, and protein powder that can be taken while on the go. Smoothies combine fresh seasonal fruit with yogurt, juice, ice, or tea.

Nothing beats fresh fruits and raw vegetables. Most people are only aware it is important to include fruits as an essential part of their diet, but only a few know how incredible and miraculous it is to include raw vegetables in our diet. If we look at vegetarian animals, especially in nature, we never see them dying of disease. Their only diet consists of uncooked vegetation. Nature offers them a great deal of nutrition per day, which may explain why they are disease-free. There is evidence that newborn babies with different allergies are allergic to their mother's breast milk and that the problem is linked to their mother's diet. I certainly pause and think when I encounter situations like these.

Today, science believes in raw food and its power to heal and cure the ailments we experience, including cancer, and recommends changing our diet for a reason. Raw vegetables are greater and richer in vitamins, minerals, and other essential nutrients. They are also low in sugar and packed with fiber that our bodies need to function well and keep our digestion running smoothly.

Eating raw vegetables provides many benefits, including helping to maintain a healthy weight, reducing inflammation, curing any health issues you may carry, and increasing energy levels. Thus, raw vegetables should be part of everyone's diet, along with enough fruits.

Watercress and Leafy Green Vegetables

It is important to include lots of herbs and vegetables in your diet during a detox cleanse. Watercress is really good because it contains all the essential vitamins such as zinc, vitamins C, E, B, and potassium. It is also a diuretic that can assist in the detox process (Narayana Health, 2013).

A Cautionary Note on Detoxing

Before you begin any life-changing diet, exercise, or detox process, you are advised to consult a physician. If you have gastritis or ulcers, detox drinks may not be suitable for you, as you may feel a burning sensation in your gut which may exacerbate your condition. When I embarked on the detox process, I encountered a burning sensation after the two-week detox. I eliminated this with aloe vera juice, which has many healing properties for the digestive system and the skin. Aloe vera, whether it is for your skin or for inflammation inside your body, is a gift-from-the-Gods potion that is always good to keep handy. Please also follow the advice from your physician if you need to.

Step 2—
Cutting Down on Unhealthy Snacking

Whatever the reason you may have for liking a nibble of something or the other, you may have realized that it is wrong if you are a constant nibbler, especially of unhealthy snacks. It is important to switch from this bad habit to a better, healthier option by hydrating yourself each time you feel like nibbling. Sometimes your need to nibble on junk food is your body being thirsty, and a glass of water may be all that you need. This is a good way to reprogram your thinking and your habits. In this way, you distract yourself from indulging in junk that your body does not need.

An alternative way of distracting you from your penchant for junk food is becoming more present, tuning into your body, and taking a deep breath. Do this at least five times when you are tempted to nibble on something unhealthy.

Junk Nibble-Free Day

Start this rule with three days a week only. By doing this, you will feel more comfortable since it will happen every alternate day. Follow the routine three days a week for four weeks. By cutting down on junk food for at least three days a week, you will be able to eliminate 42% of the junk that could already have been in your system. You will be able to feel the difference if you are taking your weight measurements.

If you want to stay healthy and fit, constant snacking is one of the worst habits you can have. The truth is that people don't "simply gain weight" as they claim. Just as they forget what they eat throughout the day, they also forget how much they eat, including roasted nuts like almonds, pistachios, or cashews.

A perfect example of how our bodies are not built in a day is the proverb, "Rome wasn't built in a day." The accumulation of so much junk in our bodies does not happen in one day. The reason I know this for sure is that I do not starve myself or completely eliminate all junk foods from my diet apart from meat, eggs and dairy and I have accomplished a healthy body over time. It is not uncommon for me to treat myself to my favorite snacks from time to time. My only concern is how much and how often I do it. My snacking days and weeks are irregular, so I remain in an acceptable weight range of around 55kg, the max for 162cm height after I gave birth to my boy; otherwise, I always stayed at 50kg, the max. Thus, you need to be mindful of what you eat, how often you eat, and how much to eat.

When Should You Not Snack?

Before going to bed.

Eating junk food at this time is the worst thing you can do, and that includes roasted nuts (so-called healthy snacks). When you go to bed, you are not moving around. Due to the lack of movement at this time of night, your junk food cannot be digested properly. There is a difference between eating fruit before bed and eating junk food right before bed. If you doubt what I am saying, try it for yourself. These experiments will yield completely opposite results, I guarantee.

Treating yourself is never a bad idea as long as you know how to keep a balance. The generations have changed, and our lifestyle has changed, but if we do not change our food habits accordingly, we will have to pay the price sooner or later.

What to Nibble on During the Remaining Four Days?

For those who find it hard not to snack, I suggest you take advantage of the four remaining days of snacking or nibbling but to do it in balance. It is always possible to replace your unhealthy snack with something healthier. However, I have provided a definitive list below as an example, also, suggesting how NOT to eat these healthy snacks. As you go through this, you will find more options and varieties of your own with being more mindful of your actions.

How Not to Eat Healthy Snacks	
Sunday	A bag of veggie chips
Monday	A fruit bar
Tuesday	A tub of dairy-free ice cream
Wednesday	A dairy-free chocolate bar
Thursday	A bag of roasted nuts
Friday	Slices of dairy-free cheese
Saturday	Cake

In some cases, these foods **still contain sugar, vegetable oil, or artificial flavor enhancers**. There is still a high sugar content in sweet treats. To maintain your new habits, **limit your treat days to one per week at most.** Once you have mastered your new rules, you will know when and how to control your treat days in the future.

Buy Healthy Snacks that contain a number of quality ingredients.

Although these treats are better than junk food, that does not necessarily mean they are harmless. Everything has its time, place, and pros and cons, so we must act accordingly. Following your new rules will help you maintain a **healthy balance** with the correct portions.

How to Transform Junk Food into Healthy Alternatives

Now you know how to eat your healthy snacks. I do not ever tell people to cut down their traditional junk food to an absolute zero because sometimes we must act according to the situation. For example, if I happened to eat instant noodles, this is how I would cook them.

Instant noodles (80 grams)	I cook this food with a maximum of vegetables, such as mushrooms, cauliflower/broccoli, and cabbies (depends what I have on hand). DO NOT ADD THE SACHET THAT COMES WITH THE PACKAGING. With this combination, I am consuming the maximum amount of vegetables while eating junk food. Add only a pinch of salt to it.

For whatever reason, if I have had a bad eating day, I would replace it with lots of raw vegetables for dinner and continue doing so the next day as well to balance the sugar I had consumed.

Dry Biscuits (4x digestive biscuits)	I combine about 25 grams of raw pistachio and pumpkin seeds with a few dried prunes or two dried figs with regular light black tea without sugar.

Below are some pointers to help you cut down on unhealthy snacking.

- Identify your personal triggers: Recognize what triggers your snacking habits, such as stress, boredom, or certain environments.

- Create a healthier environment: Remove tempting snacks from your home or workspace to reduce accessibility and replace them with healthier alternatives.

- Plan and prepare: Plan your meals and snacks in advance, and make sure to include nutritious options that will keep you satisfied throughout the day.

- Practice mindful eating: Pay attention to your hunger cues and eat when you're genuinely hungry rather than out of habit or impulse.

- Find healthier alternatives: Discover nutritious snacks that you enjoy, such as fresh fruits, vegetables, raw nuts, plant-based yogurt, coconut water, a mixture of raw fruit and vegetable juices, and freeze-dried or baked vegetable chips to replace unhealthy options.

- Stay hydrated: Drink plenty of water throughout the day to help curb unnecessary snacking and keep you hydrated.

- Manage stress: Find alternative ways to manage stress and emotions, like exercising, practicing deep breathing, or engaging in hobbies that distract you from snacking.

- Keep a food journal: Track your snacking habits to gain insight into your triggers, portion sizes, and frequency. This can help you identify patterns and make necessary adjustments.

- Seek support: Share your goals with friends or family members who can provide encouragement and accountability. Consider joining a support group or seeking professional guidance if needed.

- Practice moderation: Remember that occasional indulgences are normal and okay. Focus on long-term habits rather than perfection, allowing yourself to enjoy treats in moderation.

Remember, changing habits takes time and patience. Stay committed, and celebrate your progress along the way. Below is a summarized version of preferable snacks in addition.

- Fresh fruits and raw vegetables

- Raw nuts and seeds (e.g. peeled almonds, walnuts, Pistachio or seeds. Please cut off nuts that are high in calory like peanuts)

- Plant-based yogurt

- Vegetable/lentil dip

- Plain low-salted popcorn

- Rice cakes or whole grain crackers

- Edamame beans

- Homemade smoothies or plant-based protein bars (with minimal added sugars)

Nutrition

Nutrition is another critical aspect of maintaining a healthy body. A balanced diet can help prevent chronic diseases and promote overall health. However, changing eating habits can be difficult but you can always start with small steps as follows:

Drinking More Water

Water is essential for maintaining good health. You can start by drinking more water instead of sugary drinks.

Eating More Fruits and Vegetables

Fruits and vegetables are rich in vitamins, minerals, and fiber. You can start by adding one serving of fruits or vegetables to each meal.

Avoid Processed Foods

Processed foods are often high in calories, sugar, sodium, artificial flavors, and enhancers. You can start by avoiding processed foods, artificial flavorings, and enhancers, and choosing whole foods instead.

Cooking At Home

We live in a fast-food culture where everything is available at the touch of a button on Uber Eats or some other food delivery app. Many of us are exhausted from a hard day at work, and we often order takeout, but preparing most of your meals at home is a great way to take care of yourself and stay in good shape. In this way, you are able to control what you put in your food, as well as the portion sizes and fat content.

Further, home-cooked meals are often more delicious and nutritious than takeout. Additionally, preparing meals at home can be therapeutic, allowing you to relax and take time for yourself.

Example of a Two-Week Meal Plan with Detox

Here's an example of a two-week meal plan for detox and weight loss for a plant-based diet. The idea is to maximize a variety of healthy fresh fruit and raw vegetables with your daily food.

Week 1

Day 1

Breakfast: Spinach and mushroom bruschetta on olive oil toast.

Lunch: Chickpeas with mixed greens, cherry tomatoes, and balsamic vinaigrette.

Snack: Fruit and veggie salad.

Dinner: Soya with steamed broccoli and quinoa.

Evening Snack: Plant-based yogurt with berries.

Day 2

Breakfast: Overnight oats made with almond milk and chia seeds, topped with sliced almonds and berries.

Lunch: Butternut squash risotto with leeks and spinach, with a side salad.

Snack: Mixed nuts. Include walnuts as they are known to help to lower cholesterol.

Dinner: Grilled soya schnitzel with roasted asparagus and rice.

Evening Snack: Fruit salad with raw nuts.

Repeat the Day 1 meal plan for Day 3, and the Day 2 meal plan for Day 4.

Day 5

Breakfast: scrambled tofu with bell peppers, onions, spinach on toast.

Lunch: Quinoa salad with black beans, corn, cherry tomatoes, and a lime-cilantro dressing.

Snack: Roasted or poached Edamame.

Dinner: Vegetarian lasagna with roasted Brussels sprouts and sweet potato wedges.

Evening Snack: Fruit and vegetable salad with raw nuts or seeds.

Day 6

Breakfast: Avocado on extra virgin olive oil toast with lemon juice, salt, Italian herbs with sesame seeds topping.

Lunch: Lentil soup with a side of mixed green salad.

Snack: Rice cakes with blueberries.

Dinner: Lentil Bolognese with sautéed zucchini and quinoa.

Evening Snack: Mixed berries.

Week 2

Repeat the Day 1 meal plan for Day 7, and the Day 2 meal plan for Day 8.

Day 9

Breakfast: Plant-based yogurt with granola and sliced peaches.

Lunch: Grilled eggplant salad with romaine lettuce, cherry tomatoes, and whole-wheat croutons.

Snack: Celery sticks with avocado dip.

Dinner: Stir-fry with mixed vegetables and rice.

Evening Snack: Kale chips.

Day 10

Breakfast: Vegetable bake with whole-grain toast.

Lunch: Quinoa-stuffed bell peppers with a side of mixed green salad.

Snack: Roasted chickpeas.

Dinner: Cauliflower steaks with roasted vegetables and quinoa.

Evening Snack: Sliced cucumbers with hummus.

Repeat the Day 1 meal plan for Day 11, and the Day 2 meal plan for Day 12.

Day 13

Breakfast: Berry protein smoothie made with almond milk and spinach.

Lunch: Hot vegetable salad with mixed greens, cucumber, and cherry tomatoes.

Snack: Trail mix.

Dinner: Soya strips with steamed broccoli and mashed sweet potato.

Evening Snack: Sliced pear.

Day 14

Breakfast: Scrambled tofu with sautéed mushrooms, onions, and bell peppers.

Lunch: Chickpea curry and quinoa stir-fry with mixed vegetables.

Snack: Plant-based yogurt with a sprinkle of granola.

Dinner: Vegetarian quiche with roasted asparagus and rice.

Evening Snack: Carrot sticks with hummus.

Remember to drink plenty of water throughout the day and modify portion sizes to suit your individual needs.

What Are Some of the Generalized Small Baby Steps That You Can Take to Achieve a Healthy Body?

To start, you can begin by taking small steps such as the following.

Walking

Walking is one of the easiest forms of exercise. You can start by walking for several minutes a day and gradually increasing the duration and intensity. You can start walking at any weight; even if you are morbidly obese, take a few steps at a time.

Taking the Stairs

Instead of taking the elevator, you can take the stairs. Climbing stairs can help improve cardiovascular health and burn calories.

Dancing

Dancing is a fun way to stay active. If dancing is one of your passions, you can start by dancing for a few minutes a day and gradually increasing the duration and intensity.

Exercises You Can Do at Work

- Stand up and stretch or perform a quick set of squats or lunges every hour.

- Perform seated leg raises, desk push-ups, or shoulder rolls while sitting at your desk

- Instead of sitting in a meeting room, I suggest walking meetings to get some exercise and fresh air.

- Opt for stairs instead of elevators whenever possible.

- If feasible, consider using a standing desk to reduce sedentary time and engage your muscles.

- Incorporate regular stretching breaks throughout the day to relieve tension and improve flexibility.

- Use a stress ball or hand gripper to improve grip strength and relieve tension.

- Take short breaks to do wall sits by leaning against a wall with your knees bent at a 90-degree angle.

Sleep

Sleep is essential for overall health. Adequate sleep can help improve your memory, mood, and physical health. However, many people struggle to get enough sleep. To start, you can take small steps such as creating a relaxing sleep environment by avoiding electronic devices before bed, like mobile phones, and establishing a sleep routine by going to bed and waking up at the same time each day. Doing so can regulate the sleep-wake cycle.

Stress Management

Stress is a common experience in modern life. However, chronic stress can have a negative impact on overall health. To start managing stress, we can take small steps such as the following.

Practicing Mindfulness

Mindfulness is the practice of paying attention to the present moment. We can start by taking a few minutes each day to focus on our breath and observe our thoughts.

Engaging in Relaxation Techniques

Relaxation techniques such as deep breathing, progressive muscle relaxation, and visualization can help reduce stress.

Engaging in Enjoyable Activities

Engaging in activities that bring joy and pleasure can help reduce stress.

Social Support

Social support is an essential aspect of maintaining good health. Social support can provide emotional and practical assistance during challenging times. To start building social support, we can begin by taking other small steps such as the following.

Joining a Group or Club

Joining a group or club that shares similar interests can provide opportunities for social interaction and support.

Volunteering

Volunteering can provide a sense of purpose and meaning while also providing opportunities for social interaction.

Reaching Out to Friends and Family

Reaching out to friends and family can provide emotional support and connection. Sometimes, talking to a stranger about your issues can also help if you are uncomfortable with sharing your problems with your friends or family.

Maintaining a healthy mind is essential for a fulfilling life. Such small steps can significantly impact your overall health in the long run. It is important to listen to your body and learn to be guided by signs of discomfort as you eat or drink. I honestly believe that our bodies talk to us in several different ways.

You can become more in tune with your body by doing the following.

- Pay attention to your body's hunger and fullness cues. If you feel a hollowness or emptiness in your tummy, you could just be thirsty. Before you start to nibble on something, have a glass of water, warm or cold.

- Eat when you're hungry and stop when you're satisfied, not overly full. You really don't have to finish everything on your plate in one sitting. If you begin to feel full, stop eating and save your meal for later.

- Tune into the sensations of eating, such as taste, texture, and aroma. The experience of eating is meant to be a full sensory experience. It is almost an act of gratitude. Savor the aromas, take your time, and chew your food well.

- Slow down and savor each bite, focusing on the present moment. You should never eat in a rushed manner; it is not good for digestion.

Another important aspect of food and diet that I feel is lacking nowadays is that we need to form a healthy relationship with food. To do this I suggest you to do the following.

- Avoid labeling foods as "good" or "bad." All foods can be part of a balanced diet.

- Practice self-compassion and avoid guilt or shame around eating.

- Shift the focus from restrictive diets to nourishing your body with wholesome foods. When we restrict ourselves, it is a punishment. Exercise kindness with yourself by creating balance and giving yourself little rewards when you have really been trying.

- Emphasize the enjoyment and pleasure of eating rather than strict rules or judgments.

Mindful Eating Practices for a Balanced Life

Mindfulness is a spiritual way of living where you live in the present moment and become mindful of everything you do or say. Eating is an act that is sporadic throughout the day, with three to six meals, depending on how you choose to eat, and sadly it has lost its sacred space in our lives. In the old days, families sat down together at the dinner table and food was a social and bonding time. It was a time to come together as a family, share the events of the day, and eat slowly.

In our fast-paced world, where mom and dad are out working all day, this bonding time has become scarce in a lot of homes. No matter how busy our schedules may be, we need to make eating a mindful practice. We can achieve this by doing the following.

- Create a calm and peaceful eating environment free from distractions.

- Engage all your senses while eating, appreciating the colors, smells, and flavors.

- Eat slowly and chew thoroughly to aid digestion and enhance satisfaction.

- Listen to your body's signals of hunger and fullness throughout the meal.

- Cultivate gratitude for the food you're eating and the nourishment it provides.

Remember, mindful eating is about developing a non-judgmental awareness of your body's needs and fostering a positive relationship with food.

Step 3—
A Bit of Insight into Nutritious Food

Our bodies need certain types of food and nutrition as fuel to keep our energy levels up. We need to ensure that we balance our daily intake to maintain our energy levels. Water and fluids are a necessary part of our nutrition. Our bodies are made to process protein, fats, and carbohydrates, but there has to be a balance in how we consume these. We need to understand which foods give us the minerals and vitamins we need.

A healthy diet means knowing which foods to eliminate from our diet altogether or to reduce significantly. One of these is salt. It is used extensively in processed and fast foods, such as fried foods, solid fats, and trans fats.

I would advise you to cut down on the salt you add to your food at the earliest opportunity, because it is one of the culprits in high blood pressure, heart disease, and strokes. It can also lead to calcium loss, which can affect bone density and strength.

Other foods to eliminate are refined white flour and white sugar. These foods are linked to high-risk diseases like diabetes. According to the Dietary Guidelines for Americans alcohol should be restricted to one serving a day for women and two servings per day for men (CDC). It is clearly dangerous for our health and should be reduced. Many people have nutritional deficiencies such as low iron or calcium levels. These can be remedied if they eat a balanced diet. I truly believe that we need to know more about what we put into our mouths and which foods contain calcium, iron, B vitamins, zinc, magnesium, and vitamin D. We also need to learn about the best ways to prepare and serve food to maximize their intrinsic nutritional value.

During my 22-year odyssey into physical, emotional, and spiritual wellness, I have uncovered many unusual foods, herbs, and drinks that can completely transform persistent health issues. There are many issues that modern medical science would treat with drugs that do more harm. I have shared some of my personal experiences that have revealed some astonishing cures in Mother Nature that we encounter every day. You would never dream that these solutions could cure your bloating and make you lose weight.

Going Back to Mother Nature

A suggestion that I would like to make is that you start showing some interest in gardening. It doesn't matter the type of plants you choose to have, either. They could be anything from indoor to outdoor plants, or a small herb garden. And it also doesn't matter whether it is a large garden or a tiny garden on your balcony. A permaculture garden can be made using little spaces to grow a few vegetables and herbs.

Nothing will be healthier or give you more satisfaction than taking care of your plants and harvesting them for your table. You will have insecticide and pesticide-free food. Gardening will also allow you to draw closer to nature, and can be a source of meditation on its own. In particular, this happened when I started building my large garden and the serenity, I have enjoyed for over 17 years.

Gardening is a great way to get a full body workout, as well, and it comes with the bonus of clean, fresh air, and a spirit cleanse.

Raw Fruit and Vegetable Diet

I would also like to implore you to try a raw fruit and vegetable fast for a few days as a means to detox your system and allow your digestive system to heal from inflammation. Raw foodism is composed of eating completely raw fruit and vegetables and no processed food. This diet is plant-based and includes nuts. A food is considered raw if it has not been heated over 104 degrees Fahrenheit (or 40 degrees Celsius). You can juice, blend, dehydrate, soak, and sprout your raw fruit and vegetables.

Supporters of a raw food diet believe that cooking food destroys the natural enzymes found in raw fruit and vegetables and destroys the "living" food. Raw plant-based diet advocates believe it is a good way to lose weight, improve your energy levels, and prevent chronic diseases; not to mention that it is good for the environment and spiritual upliftment.

It is my personal philosophy that a raw food diet is beneficial to your health. The greater part of my diet consists of raw fruit, vegetables, nuts, and seeds. I swear by this clean way of eating, as it has helped me live a physically and spiritually fulfilled life.

Six Ways to Prepare Healthier Food

1. Eat raw vegetables without dressing.

2. Juicing whole fruit and vegetables/smoothies.

3. Salads (can be combined with vegetables, fruits, and raw nuts and seeds).

4. Half-cooked vegetables (can be inspired by Thai or Chinese vegetarian food).

5. Baked vegetables with a smidgen of olive oil, salt, and Italian herbs.

6. Cooked vegetables, like in a curry or soup.

As you become familiar with your alternate-day schedule, slowly increase those three days to four or five. Start introducing healthier breakfast, lunch, and dinner options, such as avocado on extra virgin olive oil toast or just extra virgin olive oil toast instead of butter toast or cucumber brochette for example. When my four-year-old son has these toasts, he adds his regular vegetables and fruits on the side. You can always choose your own favorites.

As far as I am concerned, olive oil has the taste of Divinity and the Heart of Gold. I would say the same for coconut oil. Although coconut oil contains a slight amount of saturated fat, it has various properties that fight against diseases. It is known to reduce hunger and has been shown to improve oral health, reduce seizures, and more (Lewin, 2023). It has been used for centuries in Southeast Asia along with a number of other countries, and now in the West people have also started to use this oil for different purposes.

Plant-based yogurt and fruits are always a good idea to start the day with a cup of light black tea. Having a light stomach definitely will make your mind feel lighter as well.

Make salad a regular part of your main meal, especially raw vegetables. When it comes to salads, there are many ways to make them tasty by adding fruit such as apples, oranges, pomegranates, and even mangoes. If you do not have nut allergies, add raw pistachios, raw pine nuts, raw cashews, or even seeds that will work well in most salads. In order to get the best results in both health and weight, you may want to make these salads by adding extra virgin olive oil.

The above tips definitely will work better for you if you do not enjoy raw vegetables or just vegetable salads on their own. If you are a busy individual and have no time to make salads, there are countless vegetables that can be eaten raw, such as carrots, cucumber, capsicum, Kolhrabi just to name a few and they are absolutely divine in taste.

As long as you include loads of veggies and fruits in your daily meals, I do not think you need to completely eliminate carbs such as rice, pasta, noodles, or bread from your diet. In contrast, if you replace your main course with protein from beans or pulses, which also contains a decent amount of carbohydrates, then you may half your portion of other direct carbohydrate meals. Some other vegetables, such as cooked carrots, parsnip, sweet potatoes, corn, pumpkin, and potatoes, also contain high levels of carbohydrates. If you have these as the main, you may not need any additional carbohydrates, since they will double up your calorie intake during your weight loss process.

Additionally, include protein-rich foods like tofu and fresh soybeans or long beans in your diet regularly, as well as pulses like kidney or mung beans. Make a habit of preparing a main that goes with a healthy salad on the side at least three days a week. Avoiding meat, dairy, and eggs is highly recommended, since they contain many hormones and chemicals and cause a lot of suffering to animals. Considering that emotions matter in our lives, it might be a good idea not to transfer them into our systems while striving to become healthier vision of ourselves.

However, adding plant-based protein to your food several times a week is a great idea. Consuming a high level of pulses and lentils has a flip side to it, though, as does the high level of iron. This fact is well-researched and documented (Kumar, 2021). So please be mindful of that. Thus, I am skeptical about consuming too many lentils or pulse dishes in my diet. As opposed to fresh green beans (such as soya beans or long beans), they are of greater importance. Besides soya milk, tofu, and mock meat, I also include these beans at least twice a week.

Despite this, fresh greens such as spinach, Bok choy, and other green leafy vegetables have many health benefits, including curing various health issues if you consume them in more considerable qualities. Mixing raw spinach in your fruit/vegetable juice daily will give you great health benefits. I also suggest including raw carrots in your diet regularly instead of cooking them, because when you cook carrots, it activates sugar; thus, this reduces the benefit of eating carrots rather than eating them raw.

If you have caned baked beans on toast every morning, you need to stop it. Unless it is freshly home baked. Even though this product is plant-based, it contains tons of calories, so you should eliminate this food from your diet. If you love cooking and enjoy spending time in the kitchen, you can always replace these breakfast options with other healthier options, such as lightly cooked tofu toast, roasted zucchini toast, or even spinach brochette.

Alternatively, there are healthy pre-made options available on the market. In my diet, though, I rarely eat pre-packaged foods, as they are not freshly made. However, if you choose pre-packaged food due to a lack of time, pay attention to the ingredients on the label and their quantities. Eliminate pre-packaged food that contains tons of artificial colors and flavorings with loads of unnecessary preservatives. Make sure they are made with quality ingredients in minimal quantities.

If you eat 60/40 to 70/30 (fruit, vegetables, and solid food) in your overall diet a day, you should be able to achieve your natural shape in no time. Remember to include plenty of water throughout the day and the morning routine with the detoxification process. You start with this first step, as it flushes out and cleanses your system regularly, which is very important keep the gut clean to begin with.

As I mentioned above, many vegetables can be eaten raw; below are my favorite raw vegetables that are delicious without dressing.

Kohlrabi	Carrot	Parsnip	Cucumber	Mushroom
Sugar Peas	Snow Peas	Lettuce	Long White Radish	Red, Yellow, and Orange Capsicum
Snake Beans	Green Beans	Tomato	Zucchini	Mung Bean Sprouts
Pumpkin	Cauliflower	Corn	Asparagus	Loofah Gourd
Just to name a few. Most dried beans and pulses can be eaten raw after soaking overnight.				

I have listed some healthy food and ingredients alternatives versus traditional junk food.

healthy veggie chips	v	junk snacks/potato chips
healthy fruits slices	v	candy

lemon/honey water, 100% pure coconut water, or plain water	v	sugary drinks
light black tea/coffee (without sugar), warm water, hot lemon honey water, herbal teas	v	hot milk tea or coffee
quality organic soya milk or other similar plant-based milk drinks	v	milk drinks/shakes
dairy-free/coconut ice cream/chocolate	v	dairy ice cream/chocolate
raw nuts & seeds	v	roasted nuts

Replacing some traditional food and ingredients:

extra virgin olive oil or plant-based butter	v	traditional butter
soya or mushroom mock meat or seafood	v	meat
plant-based cheese	v	dairy cheese
raw vegetables	v	cooked vegetables

Polyphenols

I discovered the importance of polyphenols when I watched a documentary. Polyphenols refer to a group of naturally occurring compounds found in plants. They are a type of phytochemical and encompass a wide range of chemical structures, including flavonoids, phenolic acids, stilbenes, and lignans.

Polyphenols are found in fruits, vegetables, whole grains, tea, coffee, cocoa, and various herbs, and this is why vegetables, herbal teas, and herbs are high on my list. They seem to be found in whole foods that come directly from the earth.

When you read the benefits of polyphenols you will begin to understand why I suggest eating as much raw fruit and vegetables as you can, and why tea, herbs, and spices are also high on my list.

Polyphenols have gained considerable attention due to their potential health benefits (Scalbert et al, 2005).

- Polyphenols are known for their strong antioxidant activity. They help neutralize harmful free radicals in the body, which are unstable molecules that can damage cells and contribute to various diseases, including cancer, heart disease, and neurodegenerative disorders.

- Many polyphenols exhibit anti-inflammatory properties. They can help reduce chronic inflammation, which is associated with a wide range of health conditions, such as obesity, diabetes, cardiovascular disease, and autoimmune disease.

- Polyphenols have been linked to improved heart health. They can help lower blood pressure, reduce LDL (bad) cholesterol levels, inhibit the oxidation of LDL cholesterol, improve blood vessel function, and reduce the risk of blood clot formation.

- Some polyphenols have shown potential in preventing certain types of cancer. They can inhibit the growth and spread of cancer cells, induce programmed cell death (apoptosis), and possess anti-inflammatory and antioxidant properties that protect against DNA damage.

- Certain polyphenols, such as flavonoids, may have beneficial effects on brain function. They can enhance cognitive performance, improve memory and learning, protect against age-related cognitive decline, and reduce the risk of neurodegenerative diseases like Alzheimer's and Parkinson's.

- Polyphenols may play a role in managing and preventing diabetes. They can help regulate blood sugar levels, improve insulin sensitivity, and reduce the risk of complications associated with diabetes.

- Polyphenols can influence the composition and activity of the gut microbiota, the community of microorganisms in the digestive tract. They can act as prebiotics, providing nourishment for beneficial gut bacteria, and help maintain a healthy gut environment.

It's important to note that the effects of polyphenols on human health are still an active area of research, and the mechanisms by which they exert their benefits are complex. The specific types and amounts of polyphenols present in different foods vary, so consuming a diverse range of plant-based foods is recommended to maximize polyphenol intake and potential health benefits.

Foods Containing Polyphenols

- Fruits: olives, berries, cherries, apples, pears, apricots, peaches, grapefruit, pomegranate, lemons, and many more.

- Vegetables: broccoli, red lettuce, spinach, potato, carrots, asparagus, artichokes, and others.

- Nuts and seeds: pecans, hazelnuts, walnuts, almonds, flax seeds, and chestnuts.

- Legumes: black beans, soybeans, white beans, tofu, tempeh.

- Herbs and spices: curry powder, cumin, cloves, dried parsley, dried basil, caraway, and others.

- Grains: rye, whole wheat, oats.

- Other sources: red wine, dark chocolate, coffee, vinegar, cocoa powder, olive oil, and more.

Fresh Fruit and Vegetables to Include in Your Diet

I have given you a lot of my own personal preferences for fruit and vegetables that are great detoxifying foods and healthy foods to eat in general. I firmly believe in including as much raw fruit and vegetables in your daily diet as possible. I thought I would include what scientists believe are good weight-loss alternatives, as well.

Pitted Fruits

A study conducted by Texas AgriLife found that pitted fruit have valuable compounds that assist with diseases related to obesity and extra weight (Link, 2020). Diseases like diabetes and cardiovascular diseases have shown some improvement on a diet rich in pitted fruit. They recommend eating stone fruits like peaches, apricots, and plums because they contain less sugar and healing compounds.

Grapefruit and Other Citrus Fruit

Citrus fruits include lemons, oranges, limes, and grapefruit. These fruits are great for various reasons, including that they are rich in vitamin C, B vitamins, potassium, phosphorus, magnesium, and copper. They also have anti-inflammatory properties, carotenoids, flavonoids, and essential oils. In fact, my four-year-old eats four grapefruit a week when they are in season as it cleanses the blood.

Although grapefruit and other citrus fruits do not burn fat, they consist of a lot of fiber and are lower-calorie foods, which fools the body into believing that you are fuller for longer. Some studies have found that citrus fruits may also protect against esophageal, stomach, and breast cancer; they contain antioxidants that protect your heart health (Wang et al, 2015). I recommend that you eat these fruits whole and avoid drinking them as juice to avoid tooth and enamel decay.

Kale, Spinach, Swiss Chard

These leafy greens should be an essential part of any healthy diet. They are low in calories and high in fiber, and are packed with nutrients.

A single cup, or 21 grams (g), of raw kale contains (Gunnars, 2019):

- Calories: 7 g

- Carbs: 1 g

- Fiber: 1 g

- Vitamin K: 68% of the Daily Value

- Vitamin C: 22% of the Daily Value

- Manganese: 8% of the Daily Value

- Vitamin A: 6% of the Daily Value

- Riboflavin: 5% of the Daily Value

- Calcium: 4% of the Daily Value

Each serving also contains a small amount of folate, vitamin B6, potassium, magnesium, and iron.

Berries and Blueberries

If you have a sweet tooth but want to avoid sweets and chocolates to satisfy your craving, blueberries will give you sweetness and health in one handful. They are packed with nutrients and antioxidants and are high in fiber.

In fact, if you do an internet search, you will find that they are listed as a superfood. A study by the University of Michigan suggests that they may assist in losing belly fat (Byrd 2016). Blueberries are one of the most powerful berries you could include in your diet as a superfood for preventing Alzheimer's. Studies have found that consuming a glass of blueberry juice daily has shown improved memory in patients (Ware, 2017). You can find more information on this topic from Dr. Neal Barnard. He has been one of my favorite doctors for quite some time.

Blueberries are not the only berries that are good for you. The other berries that should be included in your diet include:

Raspberries are a good source of fiber and also contain vitamins C, K, and manganese. Raspberries also contain antioxidant polyphenols called ellagitannins, which can help reduce oxidative stress (Robertson, 2019).

Goji berries have become all the rage in recent years. They are native to China and are also known as "wolfberries." Goji berries contain vitamins A, C, and iron. Goji berries have been touted as a great supplement for eye health as they contain high levels of vitamin A and zeaxanthin. They also contain high levels of polyphenols. One study found that drinking Goji berry juice for two weeks increased metabolism and reduced waist size in people who were overweight (Barhum, 2023).

Mulberries are my favorite of all the berries and are mainly found in Asia and North America. These plants are available all over the world, but the berries are rare to see in supermarkets for they only keep fresh for a short time. They contain vitamin C, K1, potassium, iron, and vitamin E. They also contain anthocyanins, which inhibit the oxidation of LDL cholesterol and prevent heart disease. Further, mulberries contain chlorogenic acid, rutin, and myricetin which are antioxidants and can protect against cancers, diabetes, and heart disease. It's no wonder they're my favorite.

If you do not have these berries around your area, you can always keep other berries handy; for example, strawberries. They are more commonly known in most parts of the world and contain vitamin C, manganese, and fiber. Studies have shown that eating strawberries may reduce risk factors that cause heart disease. Other studies indicate that strawberries may lower blood sugar levels, reducing diabetes Ware, 2019).

Açaí berries are grown on palms in the Amazon in Brazil. Açaí berries are one of the best sources of antioxidant polyphenols and may contain as much as 10 times more antioxidants than blueberries (Del Pozo-Insfran et al, 2004). If it is ingested as a raw juice or pulp it is known to increase antioxidant levels in the blood. There is also evidence that it reduces blood sugar, insulin, and cholesterol levels in obese people.

Cranberries have also been known to assist with bladder health and urinary tract infections in women. Cranberries are best eaten in their raw form for their maximum polyphenols as the process of juicing results in a loss of some of the nutrients. Other studies have shown that cranberries prevent E.coli bacteria from sticking to the urinary tract or H. Pylori bacteria from sticking to the stomach walls to prevent infection (Jepson et al, 1998).

Cruciferous Veggies

These refer to vegetables like collard greens, broccoli, cauliflower, bok choy, cabbage, and Brussel sprouts. Apparently, these vegetables contain a high portion of protein, and are thus especially good for vegetarians and vegans. They are also high in fiber.

Avocados

Avocados are also regarded as a superfood because they contain a high amount of healthy fats and nutrients and boost your HDL (good) cholesterol. They contain 20 vitamins and minerals including K, E, B, C, and potassium. They also contain carotenoid and lutein, which is crucial for eye care.

Avocados lower blood sugar levels and contain large quantities of potassium. Science has also determined that they contain phytochemicals that play a role in cancer prevention. For women, they contain folate, which reduces the chances of various birth defects such as spina bifida in a fetus.

I also discovered during my reading that eating avocado in symptomatic osteoarthritis patients could significantly reduce pain. Avocados are also a blood sugar stabilizer and may reduce high triglyceride levels and reverse insulin resistance (Greger, 2023). They are also good for your outside as they can be used for skin masks as a treatment for sun damage, skin tightening, and moisturizer. Others swear by it as a treatment for constipation and weight loss as it is high in fiber.

Herbal Teas

Various herbal teas have a high level of vitamins, minerals, and antioxidants, which offer healing properties if you drink them regularly. There are a few herbal teas that I would like to recommend, as I have tried them out and have had really good results.

Some of the uncommon teas that I mention here can be purchased easily at Asian grocery stores.

A Story of Mulberry Leaf Tea

In 2014, I suffered from digestion issues following a small medical procedure for fibroids. For over a year, I suffered from unbearable indigestion, bloating, and gas. I felt that there was nothing I could do to resolve this issue. No matter how healthy my eating habits were, I couldn't eat or drink much without feeling discomfort.

I was introduced to mulberry leaf tea by one of my suppliers for my ethical fashion store. My policy is to experiment with every product I sell in my store before I sell it to my customers. So, instead of waiting for the supplier to send me this product, I started picking mulberry leaves from the tree I planted in 2007. It never occurred to me at the time that the soulful garden I created in 2006 contained a life-saving herb.

After 15 days of drinking the tea, that night it suddenly dawned on me that I had not felt indigestion, bloating, or gas for quite some time. I have no idea when the issue disappeared. My research online revealed that these leaves have been used in Japan for centuries to treat diabetics, to help people lose weight, and for their abundant vitamins and minerals.

My discovery of the benefit of these leaves was perhaps not as widely known previously. My research revealed a variety of unknown uses such as the following (Kubala, 2019).

- Antioxidant properties: Mulberry leaves contain antioxidants such as flavonoids and phenolic compounds, which help protect the body against oxidative stress and damage caused by free radicals.

- Blood sugar regulation: Mulberry leaves may help regulate blood sugar levels by inhibiting certain enzymes that break down carbohydrates. This can be beneficial for individuals with diabetes or those at risk of developing it.

- Weight management: Compounds in mulberry leaves, such as 1-deoxynojirimycin (DNJ), have been found to inhibit the absorption of sugars and promote fat breakdown. This may aid in weight management and potentially prevent obesity.

- Cholesterol control: Mulberry leaves have shown the potential in lowering cholesterol levels, particularly LDL (bad) cholesterol. This can contribute to a healthier cardiovascular system.

- Digestive health: The fiber content in mulberry leaves can support healthy digestion, promote regular bowel movements, and alleviate constipation.

- Nutritional value: Mulberry leaves are a good source of essential nutrients, including vitamins C and E, iron, calcium, and various beneficial plant compounds.

A word of caution: Before incorporating mulberry leaves into your diet or using them for medicinal purposes, it's advisable to consult with a healthcare professional, particularly if you have any underlying health conditions or are taking medications.

After I added this product to my store, several customers shared similar results with me. My life has been enriched by this tea ever since.

To Prepare Mulberry Leaf Tea

Ingredients: You will need dried or three to four fresh mulberry leaves (depending on their size) and hot water to your preferred sized cup/mug. If you are making this tea with fresh leaves, then you will need to boil them until the water color changes to greenish-yellow. If not, just infuse the tea bag until the water changes to greenish-yellow. You can find dried mulberry leaves at health food stores, herbal shops, or online.

Guava Leaf Tea

Who would have thought that guava leaves could provide us with so many benefits (Baby, 2022).

- Antioxidant properties: They contain compounds that help protect against oxidative stress and reduce the risk of chronic diseases.

- Anti-inflammatory effects: The leaves have anti-inflammatory properties that can help alleviate pain and reduce inflammation.

- Blood sugar control: Guava leaves may help regulate blood sugar levels by inhibiting certain enzymes involved in carbohydrate digestion.

- Digestive health: They possess antimicrobial properties and can aid digestion, relieve diarrhea, and prevent microbial infections in the gut.

- Oral health: Chewing guava leaves or using them in mouthwash can help treat oral conditions like gum inflammation, toothache, and mouth ulcers.

- Weight management: The leaves may assist in weight loss by inhibiting complex carbohydrate absorption and reducing appetite.

- Skin benefits: Applying guava leaf extracts topically can help treat skin conditions like acne, skin inflammation, and wound healing.

- Hair health: Guava leaves can promote hair growth, reduce hair loss, and improve scalp health when used as a hair rinse or in hair care products.

It's important to note that while guava leaves have potential health benefits, more research is needed to fully understand their effects and determine optimal usage.

Preparation of Guava Leaf Tea

Guava leaf tea can be prepared by crushing six to eight fresh leaves to release oil from the leaves. Add them to boiling water for about five minutes or until the water color changes. Then it is ready to drink this medicinal tea.

Please remember that while guava leaf tea is generally considered safe, it's always a good idea to consult with a healthcare professional, especially if you have any underlying health conditions or if you are pregnant or breastfeeding.

Tulsi Tea (Indian Basil)

As an East Asian I was accustomed to this herb being used for colds and headaches; Indian Basil contains anti-viral properties along with many other properties, and is believed to be a queen of herbs.

Traditionally, it is taken for anxiety and stress reduction, to improve insulin sensitivity, as well to treat a number of issues and improve overall well-being.

It is considered an adaptogen, which helps the body cope with stress and promotes overall well-being. It contains compounds that enhance immune function and help fight infections, making it helpful in preventing and managing common illnesses like colds, the flu, and asthma.

Because it is rich in antioxidants, it protects cells from oxidative damage, reducing the risk of chronic diseases along with helping to reduce inflammation and associated symptoms in conditions like arthritis. It is also great for digestion, bloating, and flatulence.

Lemongrass Tea

Lemongrass tea assists in digestion, relieves bloating and stomach discomfort, promotes relaxation, and improves sleep.

Ginger Tea

The origins of ginger tea can be traced back to ancient China and India, where ginger has been used for centuries in traditional medicine and culinary practices.

Black Tea

Black tea could have a role in preventing cognitive decline, inflammation, heart disease, diabetes, and potentially cancer (Laskey & Barrie, 2021). A study published in the January 2016 issue of *The Journal of Nutrition, Health & Aging* found that regularly drinking black tea (as well as oolong and green tea) was associated with a lower risk of developing a neurocognitive disorder, such as dementia in the elderly, particularly for elderly women.

If you are looking to fend off type 2 diabetes and don't care for green tea, the black variety can be an effective alternative (Yang et al., 2014). Black tea also contains flavonoids (the compounds found in green tea and other plant-based foods), which may help lower cancer risk (Marks, 2022). A study published in the August 2019 issue of *Nature Communications* shows that a diet rich in flavonoids may help protect against cancer and heart disease.

Fennel Tea

This tea may help with digestion by relaxing digestive muscles and helping with bowel regularity. It has been recommended for people living with Irritable Bowel Syndrome (IBS). Fennel contains polyphenols, which provide antioxidant properties. It has also been suggested that fennel may help to ease menopause symptoms. You can buy fennel tea in tea bags or crush fennel seeds and steep them for a few minutes in a tea ball.

Fenugreek

Studies have shown that this spice helps in making you feel fuller and reduces hunger (Berkheiser, 2021). In this way, it assists in weight loss. Fenugreek can be consumed in various ways depending on your preference. Following are some common ways to eat fenugreek.

- Soaking: Soak fenugreek seeds overnight in water. The swollen seeds can be eaten on an empty stomach in the morning.

- Sprouting: Sprout fenugreek seeds by rinsing and draining them regularly for a few days until they develop small sprouts. These sprouts can be added to salads or sandwiches.

- Roasting and grinding: Dry roast fenugreek seeds in a pan until they turn slightly brown. Grind the roasted seeds into a powder and use it as a spice in various recipes.

- Using leaves: Fresh fenugreek leaves, also known as methi leaves, are used in many Indian and Middle Eastern dishes.

Here's how you can incorporate fenugreek leaves into your meals.

- curry dishes

- sautéed vegetables

- flatbreads

- powder

- spice seasoning

- herbal tea

Remember to use fenugreek in moderation as its flavor can be quite potent. Additionally, if you have any underlying health conditions or are pregnant, it's best to consult with a healthcare professional before incorporating fenugreek into your diet, as it may interact with certain medications or have specific contraindications.

Other herbs and spices that are valuable in your weight loss journey and those that you should include in your diet are **oregano, ginseng, turmeric, cinnamon, cumin and cardamom.**

Holistic Herbal Science Foods That Are Recommended for Pregnant Women

Pregnant women should have a varied diet including protein, carbohydrates, and fats, but they should avoid alcohol and certain cheeses. The following foods are recommended.

- 4 vegetables per day

- 2 cups of fruit per day

- Complex carbs provide high levels of energy and lots of fiber. Avoid refined carbs as much as possible. Include the following: sweet potatoes, squash, butternut, farro, buckwheat, beans, and chickpeas.

- Protein is essential: tofu, soy, beans, lentils, legumes, nuts, and seeds.

- Fats: flax seeds, sunflower seeds, and walnuts.

- Fiber-rice and oats

Getting Your Nine Essential Vitamins Every Day (According to Health Professionals)

Our daily routine often includes taking vitamin pills, but few know why vitamins are necessary. Vitamins are organic compounds that our bodies need to maintain peak health. It is essential that we consume these nine vitamins in balanced quantities to fight disease and the risks associated with it.

However, many of us do not consume the right foods that supply the right amount of these nine vitamins in our bodies, resulting in a lack of some essential vitamins. There are times when we may take too much of the same food and not enough of others. Over time, excess amounts of these can accumulate in our fat cells and become toxic; on the other hand, low levels of these vitamins can also lead to other health problems.

Therefore, it is essential to eat a balanced diet that includes all these vitamins instead of eating the same foods day after day. As such, health professionals suggest eating rainbow-colored fruits and vegetables along with legumes periodically to meet our bodies' requirements instead of sourcing these vitamins artificially in over-the-counter pills.

There are two types of vitamins.

- Fat soluble vitamins include vitamin A, D, E, and K. They are stored in our fat cells.
- Water-soluble vitamins are vitamin B and C, which do not get stored in our bodies. They are eliminated in urine if we take in too much.

Each of these vitamins has a crucial role to play in our health. I will outline briefly their importance in our bodies.

Vitamin A

Vitamin A is an important support for your immune system, prevents age-related eyesight decline, is important for healthy skin, and is linked to overall growth and bone development. It assists in the strength and health of our mucous membranes, which forms a barrier against infection. It produces white blood cells which also fights infection.

What You Should Eat: Green or orange vegetables and fruits such as spinach, broccoli, carrots, sweet potatoes, apricots, and mangoes.

B Vitamins

These are often called the B-complex vitamins, which is a group of eight vitamins. These include B1, B2, B9, and B12. B vitamins support healthy metabolism, maintain healthy energy levels and optimum brain function, assist in red blood cell formation, and can even have a positive effect on your mood.

Most vegans and vegetarians are often advised to take a Vitamin B12 shot because this deficiency could have some serious effects on the body. Some of the symptoms include low energy levels, tingling, numbness in certain areas, a sore tongue, memory problems, confusion, personality changes, walking strangely. These symptoms do not appear overnight but they exacerbate over a long period of time. Your physician will often be able to diagnose this and possibly send you for a blood test to determine your B12 levels.

If you are a vegan or vegetarian, in most cases you most likely consume enough B12 to avoid problems. However, vegans who follow a raw food diet or a macrobiotic diet or breastfeeding vegan moms may need to have to have tests to ensure that their B12 is at a healthy level.

What You Should Eat:

B1 (Thiamin)

- Whole grains (wheat, rice, oats)
- Legumes (beans, lentils)
- Nuts and seeds (sunflower seeds, pistachios)

B2 (Riboflavin)

- leafy green vegetables (spinach, kale)

B3 (Niacin)

- legumes (lentils, peanuts)
- whole grains (brown rice, barley)

B5 (Pantothenic Acid)

- avocado
- whole grains (oats, brown rice)
- mushrooms

B6 (Pyridoxine)

- potatoes
- bananas

B7 (Biotin)

- nuts (almonds, walnuts)

- legumes (lentils, peanuts)

- sweet potatoes

B9 (Folate)

- leafy green vegetables (spinach, kale)

- legumes (black beans, chickpeas)

- citrus fruits (oranges, grapefruits)

- fortified grains (cereals, bread)

B12 (Cobalamin)

This B vitamin is not available in foods for vegans or in plant-based diets as the contents of this vitamin are found in meat, eggs, and seafood products. Mussels are one of the most vitamin B-rich foods along with protein, vitamin C, iron, zinc, and all of the B vitamins, including high amounts of vitamin B-12.

Vitamin C

Vitamin C plays a major role in repairing body tissues and blood vessels with hard-working antioxidants. Your body also uses vitamin C to help with the absorption of iron, especially in plant-based foods and iron supplements.

I was surprised to discover that vitamin C plays an integral role in the synthesis of collagen for firm skin, ligament health, blood vessels, and healing of wounds. One of its well-known uses is in the treatment of colds and flu due to the boost to your immune system it provides.

What You Should Eat: Oranges, grapefruits, strawberries, tomatoes, bell peppers, broccoli, kiwi, and leafy greens.

Vitamin D

This vitamin is free because you can get it from the sun. Vitamin D plays a vital role in promoting bone health and growth. Vitamin D deficiency has been linked to several types of cancer and depression.

What You Should Eat: Fortified cereals

Vitamin E

Another great skin-protecting antioxidant, vitamin E also supports brain, vision, blood and reproductive health.

What You Should Eat: Olive oil, peanuts or peanut butter, almonds, and leafy greens.

Calcium

We all know calcium is necessary for strong teeth and bones, but did you know it can also help your blood to clot when you are injured, and it even supports heart health?

I eat a lot of raw vegetables and fruits in my daily routine and therefore my calcium stays balanced. My health care provider explained that calcium balances itself as long as we consume a healthy diet. It sounds to me that although I have had zero dairy products in my diet for many years, it has not affected my calcium levels because I was substituting it with a reasonable amount of dark leafy greens like kale, spinach, broccoli, and almonds if you choose not to include dairy in your diet.

What You Should Eat: Dairy, dark leafy greens like kale or broccoli, and almonds.

Folic Acid

Folic acid is the synthetic form of folate (B9), which supports proper growth and development as well as nerve and brain function. This is particularly vital for women who are pregnant as it greatly impacts fetus health.

What You Should Eat: Foods that are rich in Folic acid are Avocados, bananas, Brussels sprouts and dark leafy greens like spinach or asparagus.

Iron

Red blood cells love iron. They use it to help transport oxygen to your vital organs and other tissues that keep your body running smoothly.

What You Should Eat: Kidney beans, nuts, peas, baked potatoes, tofu, and fortified foods such as cereal and bread.

Zinc

This trace element supports a healthy immune system and is imperative for proper growth and healing. It's also a recommended supplement for skin problems.

What You Should Eat: Legumes (beans, lentils and chickpeas), seeds, nuts, and whole grains.

Step 4—
Full Body Movement and Exercise Tips

Physical Activity

Physical activity is crucial to maintaining a healthy body. Regular exercise can help prevent chronic diseases such as obesity, diabetes, joint aches and pains, blood flow, and heart disease. It also increases mental alertness. However, many people find it challenging to start an exercise program.

My personal opinion is that you don't need to exercise excessively or go to the gym every day to create change in your body. As I understand it, movement can be defined as any deliberate physical activity throughout the day. Bringing your body into active motion can be achieved through gardening, housework, walking at any time of the day, or through any other activity that moves your body completely.

If we look back to millennia gone by, the prevalence of obesity was much lower because people were actively involved in survival and sourcing food. This meant hunting, gathering, digging up the earth to plant, picking fruit and vegetables, and walking to fetch water from a river. All of these were normal activities in the course of the day that allowed people to maintain a fit body.

Looking at the past also teaches us that good food was scarce and people ate only what they needed to and no more. If we can take a leaf out of the past, we can learn to use our everyday activities as a way to mindfully move our body and mind into wellness.

Walking With Full Awareness

One of the most natural ways in which humans move is through walking. It makes sense to do more of this that comes so naturally to us. If you are just beginning your health and wellness journey, I recommend you begin at home with the space that you have, or in your immediate neighborhood. You do not need to get a gym membership at this point. There is really no need for any added expense at this stage. I want you to enjoy kick-starting your metabolism with small steps and including mindfulness in your routine.

Healthy walking involves paying attention to your body and the breathing process. If possible, try walking barefoot on grass in the early morning when the sun is beginning to rise; if not, the evening still awaits. As humans, we have lost our connection to the earth. We are a part of the earth and when we feel the earth beneath us it connects us. Modern living has influenced us to always wear shoes or sandals, and we rarely get to establish this essential connection to our Mother Earth and to feel the ground holding us so securely.

Your hands should be moving briskly in a left-and-right motion during the walk. Pay attention to your breathing during this time: deep breathing is one of the key processes in self-healing. When you take a deep, long breath, it activates molecules and cells which is the initial component of your organs and tissues. When the molecules and cells stop breathing, that's when the health issues occur. Therefore, it is extremely important to keep this element of deep breathing alive for the body to function adequately in the long run.

When you take a deep in-breath followed by a long out-breath it sends a wave of calm through your body and induces a feeling of relaxation, which in return reduces stress. Deep breaths draw more air into your lungs, increasing the oxygen supply to your body. This improves overall oxygenation, enhancing cellular function and energy production, and promotes rest and relaxation. This counteracts your body's stress response.

This kind of breathing also slows down the heart rate, promotes cardiovascular health, and reduces blood pressure. It engages the diaphragm and increases lung capacity.

By taking these conscious deep breaths, we shift attention away from distracting thoughts, and in this way, we become more mindful. This can enhance our concentration and mental clarity.

By reducing stress and promoting relaxation, deep breathing supports a healthy immune system and may enhance immune response.

The Benefits of Walking with Full Awareness

Walking is a low-impact exercise that can provide a number of health benefits. It is non-invasive and not as jarring on your joints as running. I thought that I would give you a list of what just basic walking with vigor and verve can accomplish for your body. It has done wonders for me and my overall health, and I deeply wish that you get similar results. If you have any doubts, below are the benefits that have been well-documented by science.

- Improves cardiovascular health by increasing circulation, reducing blood pressure, and bringing down your cholesterol levels

- Burns calories and helps you shed weight.

- Boosts mood and mental health as it releases endorphins, or "feel good" hormones.

- Strengthens bones and muscles as it reduces the risk of osteoporosis and improves balance and coordination.

- Improves digestion. Walking after a heavy meal stimulates digestion and reduces constipation by increasing blood flow to the intestines.

- Reduces the risk of chronic diseases. Walking can reduce the risk of heart problems, stroke, diabetes, and cancer by reducing inflammation in the body.

As you can see, walking has numerous benefits for your physical health. I would like to assert that walking can have amazing results for your mental health, as well. It all depends on how you walk, where you walk, and what you do and think about while you are walking.

During your walking time, you can either keep your mind empty or fill it with positive affirmations to start your day with positivity, or finish it with deep contemplation. It is important that you take small steps to change your negative thoughts into positive ones, which will eventually lead you to a successful, healthy life. It is not advisable that you concentrate on stresses from work, home, or family during your walking time. It's time to clear your head and concentrate on mindfulness.

A daily step count of 10,000 steps is recommended. I advise you to track your daily activity with a good-quality device if you can afford it.

To track the steps you take, you can follow these methods.

- Fitness Trackers: Wearable devices like fitness bands or smartwatches, such as Fitbit, Garmin, or Apple Watch, have built-in step counters. They provide accurate step tracking along with additional features like heart rate monitoring, distance traveled, and calories burned.

- Pedometers: A simple and cost-effective option is a standalone pedometer. You can clip it onto your clothing or carry it in your pocket to count your steps throughout the day.

- Smartwatches: Many smartwatches come with built-in step-tracking features. If you own a smartwatch, check if it has a step counter function and enable it to track your steps.

Remember to consult user reviews and consider the features, accuracy, and compatibility of these devices or apps to choose the one that best fits your needs.

Tracking your daily activity also keeps you motivated and helps you to stay on track with your fitness goals. Besides tracking your step score, these devices can track your ongoing regular physical activity. They record how many circuits and reps of each exercise you do. Some devices also track your heart rate and the calories you've burned, your daily sleep record, and even exercise movement in your hands and in full body movement. Therefore, investing in these devices might be a good idea.

Once you get used to your new routine, you can easily increase your steps by using your backyard or garden if you have one, climbing up and down stairs, even if you only have three stairs, or just going from room to room in your house. After you have become accustomed to this easier, lower-paced physical activity, you can graduate to more focused and vigorous activity.

Full Body Movement

It is always a good idea to start with some stretching exercises such as yoga or Pilates, especially if you are a quieter individual and love to have quietness within. These practices involve a lot of breathing techniques and relaxation that will help you understand your relationship with your body. Thus, you may start these steps by watching free videos online or by joining a live class.

If you are feeling judged or do not feel comfortable in a group setting, you may want to start your journey with Zumba or aerobics at home, since they involve your whole body. I highly recommend you watch some free videos that are available online so you can practice at home. This is especially for those of you that do not have time to attend classes or prefer your own space to practice.

There is no excuse for not getting started, as YouTube is resplendent with thousands of free classes from yoga, Pilates, Zumba, dance, strength training, high-intensity interval training (HIIT), aerobics, and belly dancing, all of which you can do in the comfort of your own home. I know how challenging it is to feel judged if you are overweight and go to a gym where everybody else is in peak condition. Start where you are till are confident. — one day you will get to something more.

Our body is made up of millions and millions of molecules and cells, which then form into tissues and organs, as I have mentioned earlier. These organs work together to keep our bodies functioning properly. Every system in our body is connected to the other, allowing us to move, breathe, and think.

This interconnectedness helps us to maintain a state of health and wellness. If one system is weakened or compromised, it can lead to a cascade of negative effects throughout the body. For example, if the cardiovascular system is weakened, it can lead to high blood pressure, fatigue, and an increased risk of heart disease. Therefore, taking 10,000 steps a day is only sufficient if you are engaging your entire body on a regular basis; at least five times a week.

You may not know this, but body movement can also reduce or cure several health issues or ailments. It is not just for joint, gastric, or chronic pain. Sometimes, science is a bit late in discovering these facts while your body demands what it requires to keep it pain or disease-free. Thus, it is essential to keep every part of your body, including organs, muscles, blood vessels, and nerves, alive with the movements.

Yoga

Having been born with an old soul, I am attracted to ancient ways of living. It may be the reason why I was so drawn to yoga in my early 20s. It has helped me to connect with my inner self and to be mindful of my thoughts and feelings.

I have practiced yoga for over 23 years, at times more regularly than others. It has improved my life, helping me to be more mindful, present in the moment, and appreciative of life in all its forms. It has also helped me to connect with my inner self and to understand my emotions better.

There is nothing better than a session of yoga to move the stuck energy in your body and to feel the breath enter every cell in your body. I believe that the practice of yoga not only makes you more flexible in the body, but creates flexibility in your being, as well.

Yoga offers several benefits as a weight loss tool, although it is important to note that its effectiveness may vary among individuals. Yoga combines physical postures, breathing exercises, and meditation, providing a holistic approach to weight loss. It enhances flexibility, strength, and balance while promoting mindfulness.

Certain yoga styles, such as Vinyasa or Power Yoga, can provide a more vigorous workout, while gentle styles like Hatha or Yin Yoga can still contribute to weight loss through increased mindfulness and calorie expenditure.

Losing weight can be difficult when you're stressed. Yoga supports weight loss indirectly by managing stress. It is an aspect of yoga to cultivate mindfulness in eating. Yoga can improve your awareness of hunger and fullness cues, resulting in better portion control and healthier eating.

Yoga also promotes self-reflection. Making conscious choices about nutrition and exercise that support weight loss can be made easier when you have heightened self-awareness.

Asanas such as twists and forward bends in Hatha Yoga, called Nauli kriya, can stimulate digestion. Weight management is influenced by optimal digestive function, which helps absorb nutrients and eliminate waste. This technique works wonders for soothing the stomach and releasing gas in newborn colic babies. My friends and family who have stomach issues use this technique frequently to calm their stomachs.

Yoga has improved sleep quality associated with its practice. Getting enough sleep is vital for weight management because inadequate sleep can disrupt hormonal balance and increase appetite. The best way to sleep soundly is to practice gentle yoga postures followed by a short meditation each evening, so you can wake up fresh the next morning.

While yoga can be a valuable component of a weight loss journey, it is necessary to recognize that it is most effective when combined with a balanced diet and an overall healthy lifestyle. It is advisable to consult with a healthcare professional or a certified yoga instructor to tailor a yoga program that suits your needs and goals.

Qigong

Qigong—pronounced "chee gong"—is an ancient Chinese art that combines a mind and body practice to bring about balance and calm. It combines two words in Mandarin: "Qi," which means "subtle breath or vital life force energy," and "gong," which translates into "skill learned through practice." In a very simplified description, it is the use of breath, deliberate body movement, and intention to create a harmonious balance in our bodies.

Let me try and explain how "chi" or "qi" works. Practitioners in the East believe that life force energy is able to flow in a body that is free from blockages. Negative energy accumulates through our thoughts and interactions with others, and it becomes trapped in and around our bodies. It can be released through breathwork and body movements.

As you learn about qigong, you will start to see that it is quite similar to yoga and tai chi. This practice is like an active full-body meditation where you are in the moment, focusing on your breathing, and in tune with your body. It advertently takes you out of the rat-race mentality and allows you to focus on the here and now.

Even though qigong is such an ancient art, there is actually a science behind the breath and movements. The body movements start off slow and gentle to warm up your muscles and joints, and promotes circulation of bodily fluids. Deep breathing calms your nervous system, reduces stress and anxiety, and promotes digestion.

There are many benefits of qigong, including lowered blood pressure, which is achieved with deep breathing and meditative techniques. Others who practice qigong believe that the gentle movements help to ease joint pain related to osteoarthritis. It has also helped with the palliative care of cancer patients to help them cope with the stresses related to their disease.

I would not advise you to do this alone as it requires an experienced Master who can be your guide. It is important to find an experienced teacher who can guide you through the movements and the breathing techniques. There are several branches of qigong, including medical qigong practitioners, martial arts practitioners, and those with a more spiritual practice.

Qigong is a great way to start your health and weight loss journey, especially if you want to begin with gentle exercise that is easy on your joints but works wonders for your mental and spiritual well-being.

Other Exercise Options

Weight loss is a common goal for many individuals, but engaging in high-impact or intense exercise regimens may not be suitable for everyone. Fortunately, there are several gentle types of exercises and workouts that can still facilitate effective weight loss while minimizing the risk of injury or excessive strain on the body. The following explores a variety of low-impact activities besides walking and yoga that can aid in weight loss efforts.

Swimming

Swimming is a non-weight-bearing exercise that offers a full-body workout while being gentle on the joints. It provides resistance and cardiovascular benefits, helping burn calories and build muscle tone. Whether it's leisurely laps or more intense swimming styles, swimming can be an effective exercise for weight loss. It is effective even if you are a terrible swimmer like me.

Swimming provides a cardiovascular workout, which helps burn calories and fat. It increases your heart rate and engages large muscle groups, making it an excellent aerobic exercise for calorie expenditure. Swimming involves using your arms, legs, and core muscles, providing a comprehensive full-body workout. This engagement of multiple muscle groups increases energy expenditure and promotes muscle toning and development.

It is particularly beneficial for individuals with joint pain or those recovering from injuries. The low-impact nature of swimming allows for longer and more consistent workouts, maximizing calorie-burning potential.

Compared to many other forms of exercise, swimming can burn a significant number of calories. The exact number of calories burned depends on various factors such as your weight, intensity of the swim, and duration of the workout. However, on average, swimming can burn around 400–600 calories per hour (Readly, 2023).

Regular swimming can also boost your metabolism, both during and after the exercise session. Intense swimming workouts increase your metabolic rate, leading to more efficient calorie burning throughout the day, even when you're not swimming.

Further, swimming is known for its relaxation and stress-reducing benefits. High stress levels can contribute to weight gain or hinder weight loss efforts. By engaging in swimming as a form of exercise, you can reduce stress levels.

Cycling

Cycling, whether outdoors or on a stationary bike, is a low-impact exercise that engages multiple muscle groups. It helps burn calories, improve cardiovascular fitness, and enhance lower body strength. Cycling can be tailored to different fitness levels, making it an adaptable exercise for weight loss.

Pilates

Pilates is a low-impact exercise method that focuses on core strength, flexibility, and overall body toning. It incorporates controlled movements and emphasizes proper alignment and breathing techniques.

Pilates can aid in weight loss by increasing muscle mass, improving posture, and enhancing overall body composition. It is similar to yoga but requires greater concentration on developing your core.

Tai Chi

Tai chi is an ancient Chinese martial art that involves slow, flowing movements and deep breathing. It is a gentle exercise that promotes relaxation, balance, and flexibility. While it may not be a high-calorie-burning activity, regular practice of tai chi can contribute to weight loss indirectly by reducing stress levels and enhancing overall well-being. It is a wonderful way to start your day out in the garden or park by yourself or in a group. It is a very mindful series of movements that helps to take you out of your busy mind and into the present moment and your body.

Effective weight loss does not necessarily require you to do high-impact or intense exercises. Gentle types of exercises and workouts can provide you with a low-impact alternative, allowing you to achieve weight loss goals while minimizing the risk of injury. Incorporating activities such as walking, swimming, cycling, yoga, Pilates, and tai chi into a regular exercise routine can yield positive results over time. Remember to listen to your body and progress at your own pace.

Step 5—
Maintaining a Daily Intake and Activity Log

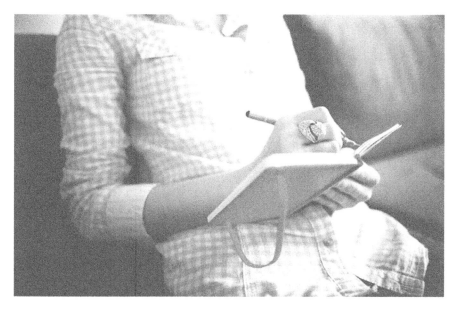

Using journaling to document your weight loss, your exercise journey, and your mental health can be a powerful tool for tracking progress and staying motivated. Here's how you can do it effectively.

Set Clear Goals

Start by defining your weight loss and exercise goals. Write them down in your journal, including specific targets such as desired weight, body measurements, or fitness milestones.

Do an audit of your mental health and all the elements of your life that stress you. Document and rate your level of happiness when you begin, and track how you feel as you go along. The factors that most affect your stress levels include your job, finances, and relationships. These stresses impact your relationship with food and the care you administer to yourself.

It is also important to record any medications or drugs that you take when you begin to track your journey, as you will eventually be able to wean yourself off some of them after you have made sufficient progress and your physician gives you the all-clear.

Your journal is your conversation with yourself. It becomes a mirror, or reflection, of what you are thinking and feeling. When you reread your words at a later stage, it will propel you to take action.

Track Your Progress

Regularly record your weight, body measurements, and exercise activities in your journal. Include details such as duration, intensity, and type of exercise performed. Note any challenges, achievements, or improvements you experience along the way. Write notes about how your body feels.

Document Your Emotions

Use your journal to express your feelings, thoughts, and emotions related to your weight loss and exercise journey. Reflect on both positive and negative experiences. Celebrate victories and analyze setbacks. This can help you identify patterns, triggers, and areas where you need support.

For example, I have noticed that I am an emotional non-eater. Whenever I am experiencing stress, I totally turn off eating. I remember, in my teenage years, that when I was upset I would go without food for three days or more, and my grandma used to beg me to eat something. This bad habit has, however, improved over time.

Include Nutritional Information

Keep a food diary in your journal to track your daily caloric intake, macronutrient distribution, and meal choices. This will help you understand the relationship between your diet and progress, identify areas for improvement, and make informed decisions about your nutrition.

You will also need to record the days you go off the rails; when you give in to temptations. I also believe that it is important to keep track of your alcohol consumption. Many of us are unaware that imbibing alcohol can also affect what you eat when inebriated.

Experiment and Learn

Use your journal as a platform for experimentation. Try different exercise routines, dietary changes, or lifestyle adjustments, and document their impact on your weight loss and fitness goals. This will help you identify what works best for you and refine your approach over time.

When you have been doing this for a prolonged period, you will be writing less and doing more. I have noticed for myself that when I started my journey I had a lot to write about all aspects of my physical and mental health. When this became my lifestyle, I did not need to write about it anymore, because it became a part of my routine and my life. Now, eating healthily and working out is an essential part of who I am. Today, I will continue to write about my emotional state and my thoughts about life.

Celebrate Milestones

Acknowledge and celebrate your achievements in your journal. Whether it's hitting a weight loss milestone, improving your fitness level, or adopting healthier habits, recognize your progress and reward yourself for your hard work and dedication.

Succeeding in the time management required to facilitate your progress is the biggest thing you should be proud of. I believe that "Time does not create us, we create time." This is the mantra I always keep in mind and work into my life accordingly.

Yes, we all have the same 24 hours a day. Some take two hours to cook four dishes, and some can manage four dishes in an hour. How do we do that? It all depends on how we prioritize tasks and focus our attention. We can use two hours and include tasks in between to produce work that equals four hours, or we could spend four hours and produce less work. Our ability to prioritize tasks and focus on what matters allows us to make the most of our time. By focusing on the tasks that are the most important, we can get more done in the same amount of time.

Step 6—
Sink In-Quietness Within

Flipping Over Negative Thoughts to Positive Action

Many of us have an annoying inner voice that acts as a Devil's Advocate for anything that we may be going through in our lives. This voice can become increasingly negative and rear its negativity throughout the day. It is like a nagging, critical alter-ego that persistently undermines your rational mind. Some of us are dealing with some really dark, challenging experiences, and it may impinge on our ability to operate normally. This increasing negativity affects the way we interact with the world.

Many people are swayed by advertisements and fad diets that promise quick fixes. They begin a diet that they have to cut out a lot of their favorite foods to follow. When someone is forced to give up something, they will feel a degree of inner resentment. Initially, they buy into the fantasy of the perfect weight, but they set themselves up for failure because they expect miracles without approaching it holistically; it requires a multi-pronged approach that identifies the various reasons for excessive weight gain. The human being must be viewed as more than just a physical being. All aspects of the emotional, psycho-social, and mental state must be taken into account.

Some of us are battling inner demons of addictions and alcoholism or substance abuse. Others are victims of violence and abuse. Some of us may be battling health issues. We are the sum of all our experiences. They shape us into what we are becoming. This book is an intervention along that path that you are spiraling off. It is a white handkerchief being blown in the wind to tell you that there can be peace and restoration. You can flip your life over. The power to do so lies within you. It takes a sudden lightbulb moment for the switch in your brain to flip.

Many of us are addicted to the constant drama in our lives because it is all we have ever known. We crave peace and long for a different way of being, whether it is to exist in a lighter, more energetic body, or to be free from anger, guilt, or resentment. To really make progress we need to investigate the reasons for our negativity.

The unexamined life is not worth living. –Andrew Klavan

We cannot call ourselves human if we do not spend some time focusing inward and finding out what is causing our anxieties. In our quest to improve ourselves, we need to understand some of the toxic emotions that can trip us up and push us into toxic habits like overeating, lethargy, listlessness, and apathy.

Toxic Emotions

Stress

It is possible to maintain a calm and focused attitude when experiencing stress. When we stress out, things go wrong—they can even worsen—and this is not the way to solve problems. Even though I know that it is easy to say, putting our focus on the solution can make this much simpler.

In our fast-paced modern context, it is impossible to escape all the many stressors that will assail us. The idea is to develop ways to cope with these stressors. In the earlier chapters, I have given you guidance on physical exercise, healthy eating, yoga, and certain exercises as ways to cope with stress.

Anger

I am aware that there are many situations in life that can lead to anger being the only solution we see. In my opinion, these occasional actions are not worth counting. Specifically, I am referring to a tendency for someone to always be short-tempered. You may consider slowly eliminating this type of behavior from life.

People who seem to be constantly angry are said to have a short fuse because little things can trigger their anger. There are numerous reasons why people become short-tempered and angry people. They are the ones who will become incensed on the road or they become triggered by small, inconsequential details.

No matter what reason leads you to frustration, you can always transform these habits into better ones. However, it is only possible when you sincerely desire to be better. If you happen to fall into one of these categories, it is better to take appropriate action now, before it is too late.

Fear and Anxiety

Fear is a natural emotion that exists to protect us from impending danger. When we experience fear, the brain's amygdala, a structure responsible for processing emotions, quickly assesses the potential danger and activates the body's stress response system.

Fear is not solely a response to an immediate physical danger. As I described in Part 1, it can also arise from psychological or emotional threats. While fear can be protective and beneficial by alerting us to potential danger, it can also become debilitating when it interferes with daily life or is disproportionate to the actual threat. Excessive or chronic fear can lead to anxiety disorders, phobias, perceived threats to self-esteem, and other mental health issues, impacting a person's overall well-being.

Defeating your problems through fear and anxiety is definitely not the solution. My personal mantra is: "Fear Kills Faster Than Anything in the World." As such, I would like to reiterate that you need to remain focused on what you want to happen for you and not allow doubts to creep in. This is the only way to defeat your fear and anxiety. You can achieve anything you desire by doing the inner and outer work necessary to shift your perspective from fear to favor and anxiety to peace.

Insecurity

As long as we remain ethical and genuine to the yearning of our souls, I do not see any reason to be insecure in life. Remember that you have a unique blueprint unlike any other, and you bring that uniqueness into the world. There is no need to compare yourself to anyone else. Every individual is good at something, and this counts from kids to seniors. There cannot be someone good at everything and another good at nothing.

Even though we may have nothing to boast about, we can create and earn to meet our needs as long as we have the desire and passion to do so. We can always give ourselves a second chance, even when we fail.

Alternatively, if you happen to encounter someone successful, take what you can learn from that person and implement it in your life. It actually makes you smarter and sexier when you surround yourself with more creative, intelligent, and educated people. If you can really see these people, do not hesitate to approach them when you encounter them, as they have come by you for a reason. Focus on what you can learn from that person and leave the rest.

Jealousy

In my personal view, jealousy is unnecessary at any stage. This toxic state of mind must be expelled regardless of the reason you have for feeling it. A significant problem with jealousy is that it does not serve anything to anyone except ruining their own lives and the lives of others. It affects innocent people who have not done you any harm.

Jealous individuals are bound to have unimaginable, unacceptable negative energy that can only be treated by themselves. We spend a great deal of our time comparing ourselves to other people. If we could take a leaf out of Steve Job's book, we would remember that our only real currency is time. Don't waste it on jealousy or envy of other people. Channel your energies into utilizing your time to focus on your overall health and well-being, which will lead you to having great experiences.

There are many ways to purify your heart and remove this poisonous state from your mind. For example, observing trees and plants and expanding your awareness with your curiosity can eliminate these negative thoughts. Watching their growth and differences in them as the weather changes allow you to dig deeper into your soul.

Connecting your feet with Mother Earth and walking barefoot on the grass will circulate your blood and make you feel light and healthier. This could be a way of transferring yourself into a positive environment. Practices like this will eventually lead you to becoming a better version of yourself.

As you become transparent with the above emotions and can contemplate, you can create a serene and harmonious environment around you and others. And stay in the quietness within yourself. I guarantee that once you begin to accept others in your heart, you will feel peace within yourself, and from this point forward, your actual healthy living journey begins. Feeling, thinking, and doing better things are priceless, satisfying, and rewarding. Remember, nothing is more beautiful than sharing your love and acceptance around your environment.

Self-reflection is an excellent way to grow within ourselves and is the only way that helps us to be better. It encourages us to be honest with ourselves and to think about our actions and reactions. Reflection helps us to recognize our flaws and take responsibility for them, allowing us to make changes for the better. Through self-reflection, we can identify our strengths and weaknesses and gain insight into our values and goals. It helps us understand our motivations and how they influence our decisions, and it allows us to change our behavior and attitudes.

Getting some morning sun, breathing in and out at least 10 times, and letting go of your worries will make your day more fulfilling. Try not to complain about your lack; express gratitude for what you have while glazing in the sunlight and feeling the fresh grass under your feet.

You can control your inner chaos by doing the following.

Quiet the Negative Inner Voice

Sometimes our negative inner voice could be a good thing when it alerts us to something we could be doing wrong that could be potentially harmful to ourselves. An example of this is driving while under the influence. Your negative inner voice will alert you that you need to stop. When we are faced with some kind of danger or conundrum, our body releases stress hormones called adrenaline and cortisol which allow us to engage in a "fight or flight" response to protect ourselves.

We need to be able to distinguish between negative good and negative bad inner voices. The negative bad inner voice is the one that will jeopardize your progress. This inner voice will whisper, *I'm not good enough, I'm going to fail, I'm useless, I will never be able to do it, they hate me.* These are the whisperings that you need to quiet and drown out with positive affirmations whenever they begin to surface. You have to retrain your mind to become conscious of these negative programs that you have inserted into your subconscious. You are the only one who has the keys to unlock these programs and release them for processing and elimination.

I picked up a morsel of astonishing information about the "Chimp" concept in an article at mindtools.com. This term was coined by Steve Peters, who alleges that we all have a chimp as part of our subconscious from birth. He postulates that it takes over our inner voice when we want to avoid doing something difficult, or if we are facing some emotional pain. Peters says that this phantom chimp has its hand hovering above a big, red button of anxiety, waiting to feed us with negative thoughts. The chimp is part of the "fight or flight" impulse of the hippocampus and the amygdala. The chimp hijacks our amygdala and controls us and our actions. It induces us to procrastinate and doubt ourselves, and it will keep you stuck to your couch watching Netflix or playing on your PlayStation for hours.

Your job is to learn to control the chimp. You need to reprogram the negative mental programming of your previous years and take back your power step by step.

How Toxic Emotions Are Linked to Specific Diseases

I have often wondered if being an angry or bitter person can cause you to be sick. I was surprised to find out that research has been done to link certain emotions to certain diseases. We have all felt hatred, bitterness, unforgiveness, resentment, retaliation, anger, guilt, shame, sorrow, regret, jealousy, helplessness, depression, apathy, loneliness, fear, rejection, and loathing, but these emotions cause the body to react in a stress response. It is this cauldron of emotions that occurs within our physical body that can make us sick. Dr. Kilcup (2015) asserts that the following emotions may cause related diseases.

- BITTERNESS: premenstrual syndrome and some types of cancer

- SELF-HATRED: autoimmune diseases

- STRESS OF ENTRAPMENT: cardiovascular, neurological, digestive, and psychological problems

- HELPLESSNESS: cancer, slow wound healing

- DEPRESSION: heart attack, diabetes

- ANXIETY, WORRY, FEAR: heart disease

- ANGER: heart attacks, hardening of arteries

These types of emotions can make you sick because of the internal stress in our organs, especially the adrenal glands that raise our cortisol levels which result in adrenal fatigue. As a result, your body suffers from inflammation. When this occurs, you become tired, and this may trigger erratic eating habits which lead to constipation, a loss of libido, and an increase in weight. Emotional stress causes more cortisol to flood the body, and this can block insulin. If these emotions are not dealt with, it can lead to insulin resistance. According to Dr. Kilcup (2015), it doesn't take long for toxic emotions to cause harm to the body. In as little as six minutes of a person being under stress, blood tests showed suppression of the immune system, and that it could take as long as 21 hours for these negative effects to go away (Kilcup, 2015). It has also been shown that excess stress can cause leaky gut syndrome and can affect the healthy gut bacteria and bring on ulcers.

Toxic emotions and related stresses can cause estrogen dominance in women, which can cause breast and uterine cancers. Other studies, quoted by Dr. Kilcup, indicate that elevated levels of cortisone in the body could damage nerves in the brain and cause memory loss (Kilcup, 2015).

I really wanted to discuss the effect of toxic emotions at length because many of us are oblivious to how our emotions and our thoughts create actual physical problems in our bodies. I would even go as far as to say that our toxic emotions create more disease than the healthy food we consume.

How Can We Deal More Effectively with Toxic Emotions?

If you really want to change your body, start with your thoughts. It is an area of science that has been overlooked for a long time, as it is very difficult to quantify or measure what is occurring within ourselves. I would recommend that you use your journal as a starting point to document episodes of high or strong emotions, what sparked them, and what you feel in your physical body when this occurs.

I suggest you use the following techniques if you want to stop your toxic emotions from becoming a disease in your body. I feel it and literally smell it every time I am under stress. It includes stress as small as trying to get my son ready for school before the gate closes. Now imagine carrying stress every day in life. Is it worth it?

Calm the Torrent

Learn to watch for signs of toxicity in your emotional body. The first sign is your heart beat will quicken and you will feel the first surges of adrenaline. At this stage, I would recommend you do not act on your negative emotions. Try to excuse yourself and walk into another room. You must learn to calm the torrent of emotions by focusing on your breathing.

Time-Out Breathing

Bring your attention to your breath. Close your eyes and feel the breath enter your lungs. Feel your abdomen and then your chest expand fully. Breathe in deeply like these five or six times, clearing all intruding thoughts and focusing on the breath. You should feel your heartbeat beginning to slow down.

Positive Affirmations

I truly believe that your thoughts can change your emotions, and in turn your physical chemistry. Positive affirmations can be used to reprogram your thoughts and bring you in alignment with a healthy way of living. The following are a few suggestions to get you thinking about words that you can use to change your negative thoughts into positive programming.

- I am in control of my thoughts and emotions.

- I choose peace; I choose the path of love.

- I release any negative thoughts and replace them with love, joy, and gratitude.

- I am worthy of happiness, and I believe in my ability to overcome challenges.

- I let go of fear and invite peace and love.

- I am strong, capable, and deserving of inner calm.

- I am surrounded by support and love, and I trust in the process of life.

- With each breath, I release tension and invite serenity. I am at peace.

Cultivate Kindness Towards Yourself

You need to realize that you inhabit this body. It is your vehicle for self-expression and experiencing the world. You need to love yourself even during your lowest times. You may make mistakes, but you will learn from them. Feel compassion for yourself.

In fact, I need you to know that "charity begins at home," it starts with you in your first home—your body. This can include exercising, dancing, singing, yoga, meditation, playing a game or sport, finding a new hobby, gardening, or writing.

Spend time doing something that brings you joy every day. I know that many of us feel stressed from being trapped in jobs that do not bring us joy. Create a small period in the day when you can do something that makes your heart soar.

Practice Relaxation and Meditation

Many of us have stopped living our truth. We have adopted a path or lifestyle that does not resonate with our souls. No matter where you are or what you have chosen to do with your life, I suggest that you take that first step toward your real self and begin to meditate. Meditation allows you to still the "monkey mind" and begin to create a space for inner dialogue. It prompts you to connect with spirit, and what you may call God.

Focus on the Little Things

We need to stop wishing for the moon and forgetting the earth beneath our feet. We often forget the little blessings in our lives. In your own body, you should be grateful for the gift of sight, hearing, smelling, taste, and feeling. There are many who don't have the ability to employ these senses.

If your heart is healthy and sound, you are lucky indeed. If you can breathe without assistance then you should rejoice. Do this every day and you will experience a total paradigm shift.

Live with an Attitude of Gratitude

Begin by learning to express and feel gratitude for all your blessings. When you begin to do this, you will attract better health, abundance, and a life of ease.

Living in an attitude of gratitude is a wonderful mindset that can bring more happiness, contentment, and positivity into your life. Take a few moments each day to reflect on the things you are grateful for. It can be as simple as appreciating the feel of the water on your skin while showering, watching a beautiful sunrise, savoring a delicious meal, or the love and support of your friends and family. Write them down in a gratitude journal or simply make a mental note of them.

Following are a few tips to help you start cultivating a more grateful way of being.

Start a Gratitude Journal

Buy a little notebook or use a digital document as your gratitude journal. Each day, write down three things you are grateful for. It can be something small or significant. By acknowledging the positive aspects of your life regularly, you train your mind to focus on gratitude.

Express Gratitude to Others

Take the time to express your gratitude to the people around you. It can be through a heartfelt thank-you note, a kind gesture, or simply saying "thank you" sincerely. Letting others know that you appreciate them not only makes them feel good but also reinforces your own sense of gratitude. Remember to appreciate all the people who you encounter in the day, from the delivery driver to the person who collects the garbage, to your boss. All people deserve recognition and gratitude.

Practice Mindfulness and Presence

Cultivate mindfulness by being fully present in the current moment. Pay attention to your surroundings, the people you interact with, and the experiences you have. When you are present, you can better appreciate and be grateful for the small joys that often go unnoticed. Many of us are always looking back into the past or wishing for something in the future, but worrying about the past and the future robs us of precious time right now.

Shift Your Perspective

Train yourself to look at challenges and setbacks as opportunities for growth and learning. Even in difficult times, there are usually valuable lessons or silver linings that can be found. By reframing negative situations, you can find reasons to be grateful even in the midst of adversity. You just have to adopt the "glass half full" perspective and learn to be an optimist.

Avoid Comparison and Cultivate Contentment

It's easy to fall into the trap of comparing your life to others and feeling like you don't have enough. Practice gratitude by focusing on what you have rather than what you lack. Remind yourself of the blessings and privileges in your life, no matter how big or small they may seem. We often forget that just being able to breathe, see, hear, or smell are privileges that not everybody has.

Practice Random Acts of Kindness

Engaging in acts of kindness can increase your own sense of gratitude. Look for opportunities to help others, whether it's volunteering, supporting a friend in need, or simply offering a kind word or smile. These acts not only benefit others but also remind you there is a lot of goodness in the world.

Remember, developing an attitude of gratitude is an ongoing practice. It may take time and effort, but as you consistently incorporate gratitude into your daily life, it will become a natural and rewarding mindset.

You may never know that just your smile could be a small act of kindness that somebody really needs. Your one genuine smile to a stranger can make their day. Such acts of kindness can lift your mood and give you a greater sense of satisfaction.

These acts of kindness can also positively affect your mental health and well-being, because what you put out is what you get back. The law of the universe is Cause and Effect and Giving and Taking.

Creating Rituals for Self-Care

You need to do everything in your power to stop yourself from sliding back into your old mindset and habits. It is advisable to create rituals for yourself so that you form long-lasting good habits. People say that if you manage to practice something for 21 days consecutively, it will become a ritual or habit.

Creating rituals for rest and relaxation can be a wonderful way to signal to your mind and body that it's time to unwind and rejuvenate. Here are some steps to help you create your own rest and relaxation rituals

Engage in the Ritual

Now it's time to engage in the activities you've chosen. Be fully present and immerse yourself in the experience. Create a routine around the activities, such as sipping a cup of herbal tea while reading, or playing calming music during meditation. Let these activities become anchors that help you relax.

Enhance the Ambiance

Consider incorporating elements that enhance the ambiance and create a soothing atmosphere. Soft background music, dim lighting, aromatherapy, or a comfortable robe can all contribute to a sense of relaxation and comfort.

Disconnect From Technology

Disconnecting from technology during your rituals can be beneficial. Put your phone on silent mode, turn off notifications, and avoid checking emails or social media. Allow yourself to fully disconnect and be present in the moment.

Contemplation and Meditation

Many people are confused about what contemplation and meditation are and if there is a difference. Contemplation is about active thinking about spiritual matters whereas meditation refers to the act of looking or thinking about something steadily and causing the mind to eventually focus on just being. My suggestion is that you divide your time between these two acts as a way to develop your spirituality and focus your mind.

You may get a bit confused when it comes to meditation. Focusing on one thing without being distracted by the noise around you is difficult, especially when you are new to this practice. This is difficult at times for many people, even for those who have been meditating for a while.

When you genuinely master how to concentrate, the noise around you cannot distract you. Or, no matter where you are, you can focus on your mind and be peaceful with your surroundings. The masters say that you can be sitting in the midst of total chaos but you can remain calm and peaceful in meditation and hear and see nothing. Your one-pointedness will direct your entire being in spirit.

To help with focusing, most meditation techniques recommend concentrating on your breathing, counting, or repeating a mantra. Additionally, mindfulness meditation is particularly helpful for dealing with distractions as it encourages you to observe and accept your thoughts without getting caught up in them. With consistent practice, you can learn to stay focused and achieve a state of calm.

Many people have asked me how I concentrate and go deep into my mind without any distractions. If I got distracted by the noise around me, I would not be meditating, as I would just be resting my eyes. Once you master how to dive inward, you do not hear any noise outside of you. I have summarized a technique at the end of this section for you to try.

There are many techniques to delve deeper into your mind. Meditation is one of the most effective techniques for understanding yourself and others. It helps focus the mind and quietens racing thoughts. Mindfulness can also help cultivate a greater connection with yourself and the present moment. Through deep breathing and relaxation, meditation helps to reduce stress and clear the mind. Mindfulness helps to increase self-awareness and practice being in the moment, allowing for greater insight into your thoughts and feelings.

By consciously focusing on the present moment, meditation brings clarity and insight into your mental state. It also helps to cultivate a sense of peace and contentment, allowing you to effectively manage stress and negative emotions. Regular practice of meditation and contemplation can help you reduce anxiety and depression, as well as improve overall well-being.

Today, the first advice given to most patients who are suffering from stress, depression, or even medical conditions is to engage in the art of meditation. We hear people cure health issues by practicing it all the time. Being a lover of this way of being, I cannot encourage you enough to make meditation a part of your life. It is ultimately a door to your Self-Transformation to a Healthy Living Journey.

The importance of taking time to reflect or meditate is fundamental to maintaining a healthy lifestyle. Health cannot be maintained entirely by a chaotic mind with good food. In addition to good food, stress, and emotions also have a significant impact on our health. Negative thoughts and emotions should be eliminated from your mind to maintain a healthy perspective.

Feeling the morning sun's rays on your body is another healing power you can enjoy for your well-being, not just for the vitamin D. As I have observed and experienced, the sun is the heavenly body that makes everything possible on our entire planet. It is essential for you and me, for plants, and for millions of other creatures. It is indeed incredible to contemplate on this morsel for a while!

Morning Sun Salutation Meditation

This is best done standing out in the morning sun.

1. Breathe in and breathe out.

2. Close your eyes.

3. Focus on your breath that is passing through your nose.

4. Follow the breath. Feel the air being sucked into your nostrils and follow its path into the body. Feel your lungs and belly expand and feel the warmth of your out breath as the air is expelled from your nostrils.

5. Keep focusing on it until you realize the quietness of your mind, the peacefulness of your spirit, and the joy of being in that state.

6. Feel the calmness, the clarity, and the beauty of the moment. Appreciate the gift that life has given you. Enjoy the peace and serenity of the moment.

7. Breathe in and breathe out... !!! Breathe in and breathe out... !!!, Breathe in and breathe out... !!!

Daily Purification Practice

Begin by finding a comfortable position, whether sitting or lying down, where you can fully relax. Take a moment to settle into your body, feeling the weight of your body against the surface beneath you.

Close your eyes gently and bring your attention to your breath. Take a deep breath in, allowing your belly to expand, and slowly exhale, releasing any tension or tightness you may be holding. Continue to breathe deeply and naturally, allowing each breath to calm your body and mind.

With each inhale, feel the release of your worry and concern. Focus on the breath passing through your nose. Discover which nostril is allowing the air to come through and which nostril lets the air out. Focus on it until you realize the peace, tranquility, and joy of being in that state. Feel the calm, lucidity and purity of this moment in time. Be grateful for the gift of life. Enjoy the peace and tranquility of the moment. Breeeath in and breeeath outtt... !!! Breeeath in and breeeath outtt... !!!, Breeeath in and breeeath outtt... !!!

As you continue to breathe, focus on the sensations in your body. Feel the lightness and freedom that comes with releasing the burden of fear and anxiety. Allow yourself to fully experience the relief and relaxation that comes with letting go.

As you scan each part of your body, way down to your toes, visualize that your cells, tissue, and organs are clean and healthy. Release and surrender all the negative thoughts, attitudes, stress, and fear into the air as you affirm the following.

I release old beliefs and habits, knowing that they no longer serve me.

I trust in my ability to overcome challenges and find peace within.

I am safe, protected, and supported by the universe.

I am capable of handling any situation that arises with calmness and clarity.

I choose to cultivate peace and joy in my life, releasing all that no longer serves me.

I am healthy, I am wealthy, and I am happy.

Take a few more moments to sit with these affirmations and allow them to sink into your consciousness. Feel the freedom that comes with releasing stress by allowing the possibilities to find you. Embrace the peace and calmness that fills your mind and body. Breath in and breathe out, breathe in and breathe out, breathe in and breathe out.

A Brief Story of My Past 22 Years Journey

There are times when I feel like I became my own healer and doctor. Being familiar with my body allowed me to gain a deeper understanding of myself rather than relying on professionals since they only know what I explained to them. In particular, if I needed to know about certain nutritious foods, or how to get rid of whiplash pain or bloating, I had to find out about these by myself.

I longed to know how to get rid of my mummy tummy, which had been wobbly and hanging over since I have had a baby, and it did not seem to go away despite exercise, skipping lunch, and eating healthy food. I had never had a problem with my weight previously. I had been one of those who needed to eat extra on purpose to gain weight.

In my case, there was only one reason for the issue: I had never been in the habit of snacking. I did not even snack on food considered healthy, such as roasted nuts, home-baked cakes, or things like that, even despite trying to adopt this habit. My subconscious mind always warned me about good and bad habits, so I was unable to change my good food habits including snacking. Thus, I am indebted to the universe for leading me to where I am today.

Over the past 22 years, I have learned a great deal about myself and my body. I can't emphasize enough how amazing our ability to heal ourselves is. No matter what the source is, whether it is herbs, exercise, or meditation, the knowledge and wisdom we need are all available to us. It is just a matter of staying open to grab the opportunity that suits us best.

This is how I survived the past 22 years after having my right kidney removed. Since then, I have lived a happy-ever-after kind of life.

Good Food

- Developing a taste for international food that is good for my body.

- Learning about ancient herbs

- Raw food and its benefits

- Making a habit to dig into the nutrition of the food I consume

Exercise

- Yoga, full body movements

- A set of self-made steps based on the body problems I occasionally have

- Keeping an active life in general

Meditation

- Contemplating the issues, I faced and finding the solution for it

- Staying peaceful within

- Embracing and accepting non-human beings and nature

- Understanding my own self, body, and mind

Applying these three habits in my daily life has helped me cure tons of little health issues in everyday life. In addition, applying these habits helped me become more intelligent, stronger, and emotionally aware. At times, I laugh when I realize how impatient I have become since I developed skills in thinking, planning, or organizing at a faster pace. My capacity has generated a new issue that needs to be revisited for improvement for sure ☺ ☺ ☺

Conclusion

"Your work is going to fill a large part of your life, and the only way to be truly satisfied is to do what you believe is great work. And the only way to do great work is to love what you do. If you haven't found it yet, keep looking. Do not settle. As with all matters of the heart, you'll know when you find it." Stev Jobs-

As we conclude our shared journey, I extend my best wishes to you if you've discovered your motivation to embark on your path to better health. I encourage you to consider incorporating meditation and gardening into your life as lasting habits. Even if you only have a small living space, there's often room for a few potted plants. Nurturing and tending to these plants is not just about their growth; it's about your own growth and self-care. It's a package deal, indeed! 😊

After 17 years of cultivating plants, I have come to realize that it's not only provided me with a bountiful harvest of seasonal fruit but also with improved health, wisdom, vast knowledge, self-realization, and inner peace. It has expanded my capacity for thinking, learning, and understanding. I hope more individuals like you find the motivation to embrace such positive changes and embark on their health journeys wholeheartedly. Remember, this journey is a personal one, and you are ultimately responsible for the effort you put in and the choices you make.

There is nothing that would bring me greater joy than to witness people like you thriving in good health and being there for their dependent children. Beyond the responsibility of bringing them into this world, your children need you because they love you. Let me conclude with some inspirational words from the late Steve Jobs:

With love and best wishes, 🖤 🖤 🖤

Steve Jobs Quotations

I reached the pinnacle of success in the business world. In others' eyes, my life is the epitome of success.

However, aside from work, I have little joy. In the end, wealth is only a fact of life that I am accustomed to.

At this moment, lying on the sick bed and recalling my whole life, I realize that all the recognition and the wealth that I took so much pride in paled and became meaningless in the face of impending death.

You can employ someone to drive the car for you and make money for you, but you cannot have someone to bear the sickness for you.

Material things lost can be found. But there is one thing that can never be found when it is lost.

When a person goes into the operating room, he will realize that there is one book that he has yet to finish reading.

Whichever stage in life we are at right now, with time, we will face the day when the curtain comes down.

Treasure love for your family, love for your spouse, love for your friends...

Treat yourself well. Cherish others.

As we grow older, and hence wiser, we slowly realize that — wearing a $300 or $30 watch - both tell the same time...

Whether we drive a $150,000 car or a $30,000 car, the road and distance are the same, and we get to the same destination.

Whether the house we live in is 300 or 3,000 sq. ft - loneliness is the same.

You will realize your true inner happiness does not come from the material things of this world.

Whether you fly first or economy class, if the plane goes down, you go down with it...

Therefore... I hope you realize when you have mates, buddies and old friends, brothers, and sisters, who you chat with, laugh with, talk with, have sung songs with, talk about north-south-east-west or heaven and earth... That is true happiness!!

Five Undeniable Facts of Life

1. Do not educate your children to be rich. Educate them to be happy. So, when they grow up, they will know the value of things, not the price.

2. Eat your food as your medicine. Otherwise, you have to eat medicine as your food.

3. The one who loves you will never leave you for another because even if there are 100 reasons to give up, he or she will find one reason to hold on.

4. There is a big difference between a human being and being human.

5. Only a few really understand it.

6. You are loved when you are born. You will be loved when you die. In between, you have to manage!

NOTE: If you just want to walk fast, walk alone! But if you want to walk far, walk together!

Some of the Best Doctors in the World

1. Sunlight

2. Exercise

3. Diet

4. Self-confidence

Maintain them in all stages of life and enjoy a healthy life.

*All quotes source from Brainy Quotes, 2019

Glossary

Ayurvedic: alternative medicine with roots in India

Contemplation: deep reflective thought

Detoxification: process of removing toxic substances from the body

Gestational hypertension: high blood pressure during pregnancy

Meditation: to focus one's mind and awareness to achieve clarity and calm

Mindfulness: state of being conscious or aware

PCOS: Polycystic Ovarian Syndrome refers to cysts in the ovaries

Polyphenols: micronutrients that naturally occur in plants

Pre-eclampsia: high blood pressure during pregnancy

Self-Reflection: serious thoughts about one's character and actions

Tai Chi: Chinese martial arts meditation and defense

References

ACOG. (2023). Obesity and Pregnancy. Www.acog.org. https://www.acog.org/womens-health/faqs/obesity-and-pregnancy#:~:text=Birth%20defects%E2%80%94Babies%20born%20to

A quote from The Great Good Thing. (2023). Www.goodreads.com. https://www.goodreads.com/quotes/8263262-the-unexamined-life-is-not-worth-living-but-the-unlived

Ajmera, R. (2018, July 23). 13 Herbs That Can Help You Lose Weight. Healthline. https://www.healthline.com/nutrition/weight-loss-herbs#TOC_TITLE_HDR_5

American Society of Clinical Oncology. (2022, February 8). Obesity and genetic testing. Cancer.Net. https://www.cancer.net/cancer-types/obesity-and-genetic-testing

Baby, D (2022). Guava Leaf Tea: Is It Good for You? WebMD. https://www.webmd.com/diet/guava-leaf-tea-good-for-you#:~:text=Drinking%20guava%20leaf%20tea%20after

Bailey, P., Purcell, S., Calvar, J., & Baverstock, A. (2021, January 18). 45% of people globally are trying to lose weight.

Barhum, L. (2023). 7 goji berry benefits backed by science. Www.medicalnewstoday.com. https://www.medicalnewstoday.com/articles/322693

Baumeister, R. F., Smart, L., & Boden, J. M. (1996). Relation of threatened egotism to violence and aggression: The dark side of high self-esteem. Psychological Review, 103(1), 5-33.

Bedosky, L (2022). What is Qigong? A beginners Guide to this energetic Movement Practice https://www.everydayhealth.com/wellness/what-is-qigong-a-beginners-guide-to-this-energetic-movement-practice/

Berkheiser, K. (2021, March 16). *Does Fenugreek Work for Weight Loss?* Healthline. https://www.healthline.com/nutrition/fenugreek-for-weight-loss#:~:text=Secondly%2C%20fenugreek%20fiber%20has%20been

Better Health. (2012). Weight, fertility and pregnancy health. Vic.gov.au. https://www.betterhealth.vic.gov.au/health/ConditionsAndTreatments/weight-fertility-and-pregnancy-health

Bleidorn, W., Schönbrodt, F. D., Gebauer, J. E., Rentfrow, P. J., & Potter, J. (2016). The healthy personality from a trait perspective: A review of the trait perspective on personality and health. Personality and Social Psychology Review, 20(4), 278-307.

Bleidorn, W., Schönbrodt, F. D., Gebauer, J. E., Rentfrow, P. J., & Potter, J. (2016). The healthy personality from a trait perspective: A review of the trait perspective on personality and health. Personality and Social Psychology Review, 20(4), 278-307.

Bondonno, N. P., Dalgaard, F., Kyrø, C., Murray, K., Bondonno, C. P., Lewis, J. R., Croft, K. D., Gislason, G., Scalbert, A., Cassidy, A., Tjønneland, A., Overvad, K., & Hodgson, J. M. (2019). Flavonoid intake is associated with lower mortality in the Danish Diet Cancer and Health Cohort. Nature Communications, 10(1), 3651. https://doi.org/10.1038/s41467-019-11622-x

Brainy Quotes. (2019). *BrainyQuote.* BrainyQuote; BrainyQuote. https://www.brainyquote.com/authors/steve-jobs-quotes

Buunk, B. P., & Gibbons, F. X. (2006). Social comparison: The end of a theory and the emergence of a field. Organizational Behavior and Human Decision Processes, 99(3), 179-185.

Byrd, L. (2016, December 7). Blueberries and its disease fighting benefits. MSU Extension. https://www.canr.msu.edu/news/blueberries_and_its_disease _fighting_benefits

Byrne, J., Davenport, S., & Mazanov, J. (2010). Profiles of self-esteem, quality of life and their inter-relationship for a sample of Australian adolescents. Journal of Adolescence, 33(1), 1-10. https://doi.org/10.1016/j.adolescence.2009.03.001

Case-Lo, C. (2017). Food & Nutrition. Healthline. https://www.healthline.com/health/food-nutrition

Del Pozo-Insfran, D., Brenes, C. H., & Talcott, S. T. (2004). Phytochemical Composition and Pigment Stability of Açai (Euterpe oleraceaMart.). Journal of Agricultural and Food Chemistry, 52(6), 1539–1545. https://doi.org/10.1021/jf035189n

Dhurandhar, E. J., Kaiser, K. A., Dawson, J. A., Alcorn, A. S., Keating, K. D., & Allison, D. B. (2014). Predicting adult weight change in the real world: a systematic review and meta-analysis accounting for compensatory changes in energy intake or expenditure. International Journal of Obesity, 39(8), 1181–1187. https://doi.org/10.1038/ijo.2014.184

Drewnowski, A., & Specter, S. E. (2004). Poverty and obesity: the role of energy density and energy costs. American journal of clinical nutrition, 79(1), 6-16.

Dr. Kilcup. (2015, March 23). How Toxic Emotions Are Making You Sick and How To Detox From Them - Functional Medicine | Chiropractic | Phoenix | Dr.Darrell Kilcup |. Functional

Medicine | Chiropractic | Phoenix | Dr.Darrell Kilcup |.
https://darrellkilcupdc.com/2015/03/how-toxic-emotions-
are-making-you-sick-and-how-to-detox-from-them/

Feng, L., Chong, M.-S. ., Lim, W.-S. ., Gao, Q., Nyunt, M. S. Z., Lee,
T.-S. ., Collinson, S. L., Tsoi, T., Kua, E.-H. ., & Ng, T.-P. .
(2016). Tea consumption reduces the incidence of
neurocognitive disorders: Findings from the Singapore
longitudinal aging study. The Journal of Nutrition, Health &
Aging, 20(10), 1002–1009. https://doi.org/10.1007/s12603-
016-0687-0

Festinger, L. (1954). A theory of social comparison processes. Human
Relations, 7(2), 117-140.

Flett, G. L., Hewitt, P. L., & Heisel, M. J. (2014). The destructiveness
of perfectionism revisited: Implications for the assessment of
suicide risk and the prevention of suicide. Review of General
Psychology, 18(3), 156-172.

Gibbons, F. X., & Buunk, B. P. (1999). Individual differences in social
comparison: Development of a scale of social comparison
orientation. Journal of Personality and Social Psychology, 76(1),
129-142

Gonzalez, K. A., & Blanton, H. (2017). Evaluative pressure and body
dissatisfaction: A longitudinal study of the impact of Instagram
use. Journal of Health Psychology, 22(10), 1330-1339.

Greger. (2023). Avocados | Health Topics | NutritionFacts.org.
Nutritionfacts.org.
https://nutritionfacts.org/topics/avocados/?gclid=Cj0KCQjw
7aqkBhDPARIsAKGa0oJHbUXg0z84pSRwXtHKWImwNR-
T9yigDpY6pp2v-ZGzx1XiXs2SxdYaAghEEALw_wcB

Gunnars, K. (2019, March 1). Spinach vs. Kale: Is One Healthier? Healthline. https://www.healthline.com/nutrition/kale-vs-spinach#bottom-line

Gupta, A., Dwivedi, M., Mahdi, A. A., Nagana Gowda, G. A., Khetrapal, C. L., & Bhandari, M. (2019). Exploring the Human Microbiome: The Potential Future Role of Next-Generation Sequencing in Disease Diagnosis and Treatment. Frontiers in Immunology, 9. https://doi.org/10.3389/fimmu.2018.03072

Hagger-Johnson, G., Roberts, B., & Boniface, D. (2013). Low self-esteem in adolescence predicts health risk behaviors in young adulthood. Journal of Adolescent Health, 52(2), 219-225.

Harvard Medical School. (2021, January 15). Genetic causes of obesity. Harvard Health Publishing. https://www.health.harvard.edu/staying-healthy/genetic-causes-of-obesity

Hussain, T., Tan, B., Yin, Y., Blachier, F., Tossou, M. C. B., & Rahu, N. (2020). Oxidative Stress and Inflammation: What Polyphenols Can Do for Us? Oxidative Medicine and Cellular Longevity, 2020, 1–2. https://doi.org/10.1155/2020/4659413

Jepson, R. G., Mihaljevic, L., & Craig, J. C. (1998). Cranberries for treating urinary tract infections. Cochrane Database of Systematic Reviews. https://doi.org/10.1002/14651858.cd001322

Jobs, S. (2005). Stanford commencement address. Stanford University. https://news.stanford.edu/2005/06/14/jobs-061505/Legro, R. S., Arslanian, S. A., Ehrmann, D. A., Hoeger, K. M., Murad, M. H., Pasquali, R., ... & Teede, H. J. (2013). Diagnosis and treatment of polycystic ovary syndrome: an Endocrine Society clinical practice guideline. The Journal of Clinical Endocrinology & Metabolism, 98(12), 4565-4592.

Kanerva, M., Soronen, J., Lindfors, P., Viitasalo, A., Saraste, A., Soininen, P., Kangas, A. J., Ala-Korpela, M., & Savolainen, M. J. (2019). High intake of saturated fat, but not polyunsaturated fat, deteriorates hepatic mitochondrial function in pigs with nonalcoholic fatty liver disease. Journal of Nutrition, 149(2), 214–222. https://doi.org/10.1093/jn/nxy260

Kao, Y.-C., Jost, J. T., & Chao, M. M. (2019). Perceived parental criticism and self-esteem: A cross-cultural comparison. Personality and Individual Differences, 149, 142-149. doi: 10.1016/j.paid.2019.06.036

Kubala, J. (2019, November 29). Mulberry Leaf: Uses, Benefits, and Precautions. Healthline. https://www.healthline.com/nutrition/mulberry-leaf#:~:text=Mulberry%20leaves%20may%20help%20lower

Kumar, K. (2021, September 9). Why Are Lentils Bad for You? MedicineNet; MedicineNet. https://www.medicinenet.com/why_are_lentils_bad_for_you/article.htm

Kureshi, A; Khalak, R; Gifford, J; Munshi . (2022) Maternal Obesity-Associated Neonatal Morbidities in Early Newborn Period. https://www.frontiersin.org/articles/10.3389/fped.2022.867171/full#:~:text=Infants%20born%20to%20obese%20mothers%20are%20more%20likely%20to%20be,in%20the%20early%20neonatal%20period.

Laskey, J., & Barrie, L. (2021, February 12). 8 Teas to Drink for a Healthier Body and Mind| Everyday Health. EverydayHealth.com. https://www.everydayhealth.com/diet-nutrition/diet/best-teas-your-health/

Lee, E. E., Tripp-Reimer, T., Miller, A. M., Sadler, G. R., & Lee, J. Y. (2014). Korean American women's experiences with cultural attitudes toward appearance. Journal of Transcultural Nursing, 25(1), 52-60. doi:10.1177/1043659613488431

Lewin, J. (2023). The health benefits of coconut oil. BBC Good Food. https://www.bbcgoodfood.com/howto/guide/health-benefits-coconut-oil

Link, R. (2018, July 23). 13 Herbs That Can Help You Lose Weight. Healthline; Healthline Media. https://www.healthline.com/nutrition/weight-loss-herbs

Link, R. (2020). Top 16 Stone Fruit You Should Eat. Dr. Axe. https://draxe.com/nutrition/stone-fruit/

Loos, R. J. F., & Yeo, G. S. H. (2014). The genetics of obesity: What have we learned? In International Journal of Obesity (Vol. 38, Issue 1, pp. 7–12)._Mruk, C. (2018). Self-esteem research, theory, and practice: Toward a positive psychology of self-esteem (4th ed.). New York, NY: Springer. https://doi.org/10.1038/ijo.2014.184

Mayo Clinic Staff. (2022) Pregnancy and Obesity: Know the Risks. https://www.mayoclinic.org/healthy-lifestyle/pregnancy-week-by-week/in-depth/pregnancy-and-obesity/art-20044409

Marks, J. L. (2022). Cancer Risk Factors. EverydayHealth.com. https://www.everydayhealth.com/cancer/guide/cancer-risk-factors-prevention/

Mason, S. M., Flint, A. J., Field, A. E., Austin, S. B., & Rich-Edwards, J. W. (2020). Abuse victimization in childhood or adolescence and risk of food addiction in adult women. Obesity, 28(3), 573-581. doi: 10.1002/oby.22751

Mruk, C. (2018). Self-esteem research, theory, and practice: Toward a positive psychology of self-esteem (4th ed.). New York, NY: Springer.

Narayana Health. (2013, October 25). Detox Foods : Detoxification is an essential part of optimal health. Narayana Health Care; Narayana Health Care. https://www.narayanahealth.org/blog/detox-foods-detoxification-is-an-essential-part-of-optimal-health/

National Institute of Health. (2019). Talking Glossary of Genetic Terms | NHGRI. Www.genome.gov. https://www.genome.gov/genetics-glossary/Obesity

National Institutes of Health. (2019). Obesity and genetics. https://www.genome.gov/genetics-glossary/Obesity

Netmed. (2022). 5 Incredible Home Remedies For Fatty Liver And To Enhance Liver Health. Netmeds. https://www.netmeds.com/health-library/post/5-incredible-home-remedies-for-fatty-liver-and-to-enhance-liver-health#:~:text=Apple%20Cider%20Vinegar&text=Incredible%20detoxification%20actions%20of%20ACV

Oosterhoff, B., Kaplow, J. B., & Layne, C. M. (2018). Trajectories of posttraumatic stress and depressive symptoms in adolescent girls: A comparison of symptom profiles. Journal of Affective Disorders, 234, 114-120.

Pandey, K. B., & Rizvi, S. I. (2009). Plant polyphenols as dietary antioxidants in human health and disease. Oxidative Medicine and Cellular Longevity, 2(5), 270-278. doi: 10.4161/oxim.2.5.9498

Robertson, R. (2019, September 17). The 8 Healthiest Berries You Can Eat. Healthline. https://www.healthline.com/nutrition/8-healthy-berries

Readly. (2023). *How Many Calories Does Swimming Burn? The Benefits of Swimming for Weight Loss* - Readly. Gb.readly.com. https://gb.readly.com/spotlight/running-cycling-fitness/how-

many-calories-does-swimming-burn-the-benefits-of-swimming-
for-weight-
loss#:~:text=Swimming%20is%20proven%20to%20burn

Sánchez-Villegas, A., Madrigal, H., Hininger-Favier, I., Cassan, D., &
Tresserra-Rimbau, A. (2018). Childhood trauma and disordered
eating behaviors: A systematic review and meta-analysis.
Nutrients, 10(10), 1-18. doi: 10.3390/nu10101546

Scalbert, A., Johnson, I. T., & Saltmarsh, M. (2005). Polyphenols:
Antioxidants and beyond. The American Journal of Clinical
Nutrition, 81(1 Suppl), 215S-217S. doi: 10.1093/ajcn/81.1.215s

Schüssler-Fiorenza Rose, S. M., Xie, D., & Stineman, M. G. (2019).
Adverse childhood experiences and obesity: Systematic review
of behavioral interventions targeting obesity among individuals
with adverse childhood experiences. Obesity Reviews, 20(8),
1149-1165. doi: 10.1111/obr.12853

Schneider, S. K., O'Donnell, L., Stueve, A., & Coulter, R. W. S. (2012).
Cyberbullying, school bullying, and psychological distress: A
regional census of high school students. American Journal of
Public Health, 102(1), 171-177.

Sermondade, N., Faure, C., Fezeu, L., Shayeb, A. G., Bonde, J. P.,
Jensen, T. K., ... & Czernichow, S. (2013). BMI in relation to
sperm count: an updated systematic review and collaborative
meta-analysis. Human Reproduction Update, 19(3), 221-231.

Sonstroem, R. J., & Morgan, W. P. (1989). Exercise and self-esteem:
Rationale and model. Medicine and Science in Sports and
Exercise, 21(3), 329-337.

Sroufe, L. A., Egeland, B., Carlson, E. A., & Collins, W. A. (2005). The
development of the person: The Minnesota study of risk and
adaptation from birth to adulthood. Guilford Press.

Suls, J., Martin, R., & Wheeler, L. (2002). Social comparison: Why, with whom, and with what effect? Current Directions in Psychological Science, 11(5), 159-163.

Tesser, A. (2018). Self-evaluation maintenance theory. In H. T. Reis & S. K. Sprecher (Eds.), Encyclopedia of human relationships (2nd ed., pp. 1759-1762). Hoboken, NJ: John Wiley & Sons.

Tesser, A. (2018). Self-evaluation maintenance theory. In H. T. Reis & S. K. Sprecher (Eds.), Encyclopedia of human relationships (2nd ed., pp. 1759-1762). Hoboken, NJ: John Wiley & Sons.Manzoor, S., Naz, R., & Chaudhary, F. M. (2021). Detoxification in healthy individuals: A randomized controlled trial on oxidative stress, inflammation and liver function. Pakistan Journal of Medical Sciences, 37(1), 49-54. https://doi.org/10.12669/pjms.37.1.3237

Trzesniewski, K. H., Donnellan, M. B., & Robins, R. W. (2006). Stability of self-esteem across the life span. Journal of Personality and Social Psychology, 91(4), 644-659. https://doi.org/10.1037/0022-3514.91.4.644

Ttofi, M. M., & Farrington, D. P. (2011). Effectiveness of school-based programs to reduce bullying: A systematic and meta-analytic review. Journal of Experimental Criminology, 7(1), 27-56.

U.S. National Library of Medicine. (2022, March 3). Genetic obesity syndromes. MedlinePlus. https://medlineplus.gov/genetics/condition/genetic-obesity-syndromes/

Wang, A., Zhu, C., Fu, L., Wan, X., Yang, X., Zhang, H., Miao, R., He, L., Sang, X., & Zhao, H. (2015). Citrus Fruit Intake Substantially Reduces the Risk of Esophageal Cancer. Medicine, 94(39). https://doi.org/10.1097/MD.0000000000001390

Ware, M. (2017, September 5). Blueberries: Health benefits, facts, and research. Www.medicalnewstoday.com. https://www.medicalnewstoday.com/articles/287710#:~:text=They%20have%20been%20shown%20to

Ware, M. (2017, September 5). Blueberries: Health benefits, facts, and research. Www.medicalnewstoday.com. https://www.medicalnewstoday.com/articles/287710#:~:text=They%20have%20been%20shown%20to

Ware, M. (2019, May 29). Strawberries: Benefits, nutrition, and risks. Www.medicalnewstoday.com. https://www.medicalnewstoday.com/articles/strawberries#:~:text=Strawberries%20might%20help%20protect%20against

Wilson, S., Durbin, C. E., Fergusson, D. M., & Horwood, L. J. (2010). Life course perspectives on the vulnerability of children and adults to episodes of depression and anxiety. In K. Kiernan & H. A. Schurer (Eds.), Dynamics of inequality and poverty (pp. 149-171). Oxford University Press.

Wood, J. V., Heimpel, S. A., & Michela, J. L. (2003). Savoring versus dampening: Self-esteem differences in regulating positive affect. Journal of Personality and Social Psychology, 85(3), 566-580.

Yang, J., Mao, Q.-X. ., Xu, H.-X. ., Ma, X., & Zeng, C.-Y. . (2014). Tea consumption and risk of type 2 diabetes mellitus: a systematic review and meta-analysis update. BMJ Open, 4(7), e005632–e005632. https://doi.org/10.1136/bmjopen-2014-005632\

Image References

Falconp4 Tea, Kettle, Teapot https://pixabay.com/photos/tea-kettle-teapot-drink-cup-2776217/

Gabriele Bartoletti stella Fruit and Vegetable Composition https://unsplash.com/photos/hhlF006622M

Ha11ok Gymnast stick man https://pixabay.com/vectors/gymnast-stick-man-man-stick-2353968/

JillWellington Woman, Silhouette, Sunset https://pixabay.com/photos/woman-silhouette-sunset-beach-sea-570883/

Kent, Todd (2022) Sunshine https://unsplash.com/photos/PsLrgT55DeM

Krukau, Jan https://www.pexels.com/photo/cheerful-sportswoman-meditating-in-lotus-pose-with-son-4457982/

Marco, P Yoga, yoga, yoga pose asanahttps://pixabay.com/photos/yoga-yoga-pose-asana-sunset-woman-5281457/

Picjumbo_com Female diary journal https://pixabay.com/photos/female-diary-journal-write-865110/

Raic,V. Tape, Tomato, Glas https://pixabay.com/photos/tape-tomato-glas-diet-water-403592/

RitaE Elder Blossoms, syrup https://pixabay.com/photos/elder-blossoms-syrup-bottles-vial-2381616/

Sofia_Schulz_Photography Sisters, Love, Hugs https://pixabay.com/photos/sisters-hug-love-friends-girls-6274743/

Made in the USA
Coppell, TX
07 June 2024

33207708R00089